# CHARTING THE COURSE

# CHARTING THE COURSE

## *A Workbook on Christian Discipleship*

TERESA GILBERT

PATTY JOHANSEN

JAY REGENNITTER

WITH JOHN P. GILBERT

DISCIPLESHIP RESOURCES

PO BOX 340003 • NASHVILLE, TN 37203-0003
www.discipleshipresources.org

ISBN 978-0-88177-507-5

Library of Congress Control Number 2007929199

# TABLE OF CONTENTS

# INTRODUCTION

You have this workbook because you have discerned one of two things: your church could benefit from the development of a disciple formation process that is unique to your congregation's context; or your church is already involved in discipleship ministries but needs to form more of a process or flow to help people grow deeper in faith. We believe that a disciple formation process can help congregations make and grow disciples of Jesus Christ, in fulfillment of his mission to us. (Matt 28:19-20)

A disciple formation process can

- help individuals understand exactly what a disciple is.

- help individuals understand that a life of discipleship is a lifelong journey.

- help individuals know specific things they can do to grow deeper as a disciple of Jesus Christ.

- help answer the question that many churches are asking, "How do we fulfill what Jesus commanded? How do we make and grow disciples?"

- let the community know that the church is taking seriously the call to make disciples.

## What is *Charting the Course* all about?

*Charting the Course* is a process for local churches to initiate intentional leadership development and intentional disciple formation. *Charting the Course* is a response to the question churches are asking, which is, "We really want to be about forming disciples for Jesus Christ, but how do we do that?" This study helps churches to:

- develop leaders who practice the means of grace in their own lives and teach others to do the same, and

- design a disciple-formation process within their own congregation that is contextually relevant to their situation.

## What is this book about?

This is a Discipleship Workbook. Whether you are a layperson, pastor, committee chair, or staff member, the whole purpose of this book is to involve you and your congregation in

1.) understanding just what making disciples is and involves,

2.) evaluating your present efforts at making disciples, and

3.) planning specific disciple-making ministries for the future.

So this is not a book to be read alone! This is a workbook to be read, discussed, and used by many persons in your congregation at the same time.

## So Who Should Be Reading and Discussing This Book?

- If yours is a small congregation, why not the whole congregation?

- Perhaps the Administrative Council, or Council on Ministries, or whatever title you give to the group that is responsible for the ministries of your congregation.

- How about an adult Sunday School class? Or several adult Sunday School classes, and perhaps a youth class or two thrown in as well?

- A weeknight study group of folks drawn from your congregation? Or how about inviting interested folks from a neighboring congregation or two to join with you?

- The United Methodist Women and United Methodist Men? These folks are often the "movers and shakers" in our congregation.

- An *ad hoc* group of committed persons drawn together just for this purpose?

- If yours is a really large-membership congregation, how about the staff of the church working through this book before involving key laypersons in the study?

We hope you're getting the point here. The more persons you can involve in this study and discussion, the better!

## But Who's Going to Lead or Facilitate the Study and Discussion of This Workbook?

Good question! The leader or facilitator must be one who is committed to the church, already an active disciple, passionate about the mission of the congregation, a "people person," a conciliator and reconciler, and an enthusiastic and tenacious individual! Does this mean the pastor? Not necessarily. In fact, a strong lay leader might encourage more persons to become involved and "catch the idea" better than the pastor (who, unfortunately, might be seen as "pushing the latest program that's come down the pipeline"). Of course, the pastor must be involved every step of the way, but assuming that the pastor is the only one who can facilitate the study and use of this workbook is to deny the great talent, commitment, and enthusiasm resident among the lay members of our congregation—even if that congregation consists of only ten individuals!

So gather the groups and work through this book together!

## Some Comments about a Group Study of This Book

- Set a time for study sessions. Start on time, and end at the promised time.

- Surround every session with prayer! Begin every session with prayer, and end every session with prayer. And if the group seems to reach an impasse, pray! Let group members offer prayers. Call for silent prayer. But surround your sessions with prayer.

- Set up your meeting room so that all can see one another. Pews in the nave do not work well for this kind of discussion.

- Have a chalkboard, white board, and/or newsprint available. Use it!

- Ask at least one person to take notes on your discussions. Better if two or three take notes. That way, each can contribute to the discussion as well as note-taking. Don't try to "combine" the notes into one set of minutes. Hear from each note-taker at the end of a session and at the beginning of the next session. The richness of your discussion will be revealed!

- Make decisions, then move on! Try to make decisions by consensus; that is, an idea or decision is discussed until everyone "buys into it." Voting creates winners and losers. By working toward consensus, everyone wins!

- Two little clichés worth remembering: 1.) *Once you give an idea to the group, the idea belongs to the group, not to you anymore.* The group can change, adapt, accept, or reject the idea because the idea now belongs to the group. 2.) *A group can get anything done that needs to be done as long as no one cares who gets credit for it!*

## About this Guide

### CENTERING PRAYER

Each section of this guide will begin with a centering prayer. We've used this prayer both for individual preparation prior to a team meeting, and to center the team and/or congregation during gatherings.

### CHAPTER AT A GLANCE

The Chapter at a Glance section lists the goals, time frame, format, and suggestions for that particular chapter's activities.

### INDIVIDUAL PREPARATION

Each team member should read each chapter individually prior to coming to the meeting for that session's work.

### ROLE OF TEAM

When we say "the team", we are referring to the initial group that began this disciple-formation process. At times throughout your work together, the team may need to take a specific role in guiding the congregation.

### ROLE OF PASTOR

This process will require cooperation from the clergy and lay leadership of your church to enter into this process. The pastor is in a strategic position to remind the whole congregation of the Church's mission.

## CHECK THE EMOTIONAL CLIMATE

The team will do well to select a person or persons to continue checking the emotional climate and to help remind the congregation of the mission and vision. This guidance may mean that the process slows down some, but the hearts and minds of people and the mission are worth this careful attention.

**A Word of Caution**: It should be understood that the person(s) assigned to this role should not be expected to "have all the answers" when frustration, confusion, and/or problems arise. The role of this person(s) is to make the team aware of the current climate, and the team will collectively make decisions about how to best address situations, including the possiblity of inviting an outside person skilled in team building to work with the team for one or more sessions; for example, scheduling a meeting with that group to dialogue openly, or gathering additional information that is needed to address any potential conflicts.

## GOING DEEPER, ADDITIONAL RESOURCES, AND BIBLE STUDY

If your congregation wants to explore more in a chapter or to take more time with a particular topic, we've included a "Going Deeper" section, which may include additional exercises, Bible studies, and/or a listing of resources.

## HANDOUTS

Handouts can be found either at the end of the chapter or at the back of the book for your convenience in leading your team.

## BEFORE MOVING ON

This section contains helpful suggestions in one's preparation for the next chapter.

## How Long Is the Study?

This workbook is set up for about nine two-hour sessions. Some congregations might go through more quickly; others might take a little more time. But keep in mind that groups get "burned out" or tired if a study like this is stretched over too long a period of time. We suggest a period of three to twelve months, depending on your local situation.

We believe that the development of a disciple-formation process in a local church can quench thirsting spirits, fill souls with living water, and aid your congregation in effectively fulfilling its mission. As the Holy Spirit guides and directs your church, let this study help chart your course as you develop and carry out an intentional, ongoing plan for forming disciples in your unique context.

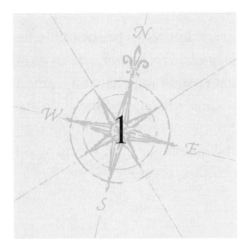

# WE'RE ON A MISSION!

The aim of this chapter is to help the congregation embrace disciple making as a mission. This is a chance for the congregation to grow in its understanding of the mission of the United Methodist Church and how the disciple-formation process will flow from that mission.

## Centering Prayer

*Great and amazing God, as we begin a process of discernment, may you lead us in making our work worshipful throughout our time together. As we focus and gain perspective on who you call us to be, and as we seek to reclaim the mission of making disciples, may you embrace us. Keep us grounded in what your word has to say to us during our time together. May you be the focus of all that we say and do. We pray in the name of the one who gave us the Great Commission, Jesus the Christ. Amen.*

## Chapter at a Glance

### GOALS

- To understand that making disciples is the biblical mission of every church.

- To find ways to help your congregation embrace this mission.

- To develop a team to lead your congregation by creating an intentional disciple-formation process that will be transformational in your church and community.

## TIMEFRAME SUGGESTIONS

You might first want to ask the lead pastor and two to four lay leaders to brainstorm who should make up the team. This group should have read workbook in its entirety. If it is clear who should be on the team, meet and work through the first chapter together as a team. If the team decision is not clear, determine next steps for deciding who should make up the team. The team should meet together once or twice for the sole purpose of building relationships, studying the mission of the Church together, and creating a spirit of unity. All team members should read the entire workbook before proceeding together.

## POSSIBLE FORMAT

- Read the centering prayer together, or have the facilitator read while the group meditates.

- Discuss thoughts about chapter 1

- Group Reflection Time

  ■ Allow each participant to respond to the statements below; allow 5-10 minutes for each statement: (Capture thoughts on newsprint for future reference)

    — "The (*Discipline* statement) does not read 'A mission . . . ' or 'One of the missions . . . ' The statement reads loudly and clearly that the one, single, exclusive mission of the Church is to make disciples of Jesus Christ."

    — "Put most simply and directly, a mission is what we are supposed to be doing and what we are to do. Our mission is our reason for being. It is the cause for which we exist."

    — "Our mission is what we are given to do by a higher authority. Our mission is not something we choose or define or modify. Our mission is not optional. The higher authority is not *The Book of Discipline of The United Methodist Church*, or the General Conference of the United Methodist Church, or a group of bishops. That higher authority is God through Christ. It is God through Christ who gives us our mission."

- Read or have read Matthew 28:16-20.

- The facilitator will ask questions to the group: (Capture answers to questions on newsprint)

- ■ As we begin this journey together, what are your initial thoughts about our congregation?

- ■ If our mission is to do all we can to make, form, and shape others into disciples of Jesus Christ, is our congregation actively engaged in making disciples?

- ■ Are the folks who make up our congregation disciples themselves?

- ■ How do we move our congregation to be more focused on disciple-making? (This question should generate lots of thoughts and ideas).

- • Read or have read Matthew 28:16-20 again.

- • Close in prayer, in whatever way seems appropriate.

- • Note: Any chapter may take more than one session to adequately complete. Proceed at your own pace.

## Individual Preparation

> The mission of the Church is to make disciples of Jesus Christ. Local churches provide the most significant arena through which disciple-making occurs. *The Book of Discipline of The United Methodist Church, 2004*; ¶120 (p. 87).

Wait!!

Go back and read what's in that box just above. You might have read it dozens of times before. But read it again. Read it slowly. Read it aloud. Read it again.

Now let's take a careful look at that statement, because each word is crucial.

The first word is *The*. Yes, we all know what that word means. But in this sentence that word carries a special meaning that we might miss. The sentence does not read "*A* mission" or "*One of the* missions." No, the statement reads loudly and clearly that the *one, single, exclusive* mission of the Church is to make disciples of Jesus Christ.

What about the second word: *mission*? What is a mission? Put most simply and directly, a mission is what we are supposed to be doing and what we are to do. Our mission is our reason for being. It is the cause for which we exist. It is the way we are to be spending ourselves. Our mission is the reason why we are here. Our mission is what we are about. Our mission is what we are given to do by a higher authority. Our mission is not something we choose or define or modify. Our mission is given to us and we are charged with and held responsible for fulfilling that mission. Our mission is not optional. Either we undertake our mission joyfully and enthusiastically or we fail completely and endure the consequences of our failure.

Back up a minute: Did you catch the sentence in the previous paragraph that says our mission is given to us by a higher authority? That higher authority is not *The Book of Discipline of The United Methodist Church* or the General Conference of The United Methodist Church or a group of bishops. That higher authority is God through Christ. It is God through Christ who gives us our mission. The United Methodist Church may put that mission into a set of words, but the mission is given to us by God. The Church did not select or choose this mission. God through Christ charged the Church with this mission. Matthew 28:18-20 is but one of many, many passages of Scripture that could be cited to demonstrate this.

Whose mission is it? The Church's. Note that the word "Church" is capitalized in this statement.

- That suggests that the Church on every level and in every form is charged with this mission.

- That means that the Church, not matter how we define it, has this as its mission.

- That means that the huge cathedral, the tiny rural frame building, the established congregation in the suburb, the little group of folks meeting in a storefront in the inner city, the new congregation that is just beginning to grow, the handful of related folks who have always called that crossroads building their church – all of these and every other example you can imagine – share in one common mission, one common calling, one common task given them by God through Christ.

The Church, as a body of believers in Christ, does not choose its mission, does not decide whether or not it will accept this mission. Instead, one definition of the Church is that *the Church is a group of persons committed to fulfilling the mission given to those persons by God.*

And what is that mission?

### *Our mission is to make disciples of Jesus Christ.*

Now we can quibble all we want over that verb *make*. That word does not mean that we "make" disciples as we would make a pie or a birdhouse. That word *make* means in this case that our mission, our task, the reason we are here, is to create those situations, those environments, and those conditions in and through which other persons can come to know Christ and live according to the way of Christ.

Our mission is to do all we can to make, form, and shape others into disciples of Jesus Christ.

OK. What is a *disciple*?

That is a very big and a very important question! And we are going to devote a major section of this workbook to determining a functional definition of the word *disciple*. (A functional definition is a definition that describes what something *does*, not just what something *is*. Watch for it. Disciples are persons who do and act in certain ways; they are not persons who just say "yes" to something, then go their own way.) In this case we are talking about disciples of Jesus Christ, so these disciples will in some way do and act like Jesus. We'll explore that picture more in the next chapter.

And the rest of the statement in the box? That entire second sentence is a fancy way of saying that each congregation (not a church building but congregation; that is, a group of people!) —be its membership five or ten or one hundred or one thousand or ten thousand—is the prime place, the major place, the most important place in and through which persons come to be disciples. The mission is not carried out by a building; the mission is carried out by persons! And we call a group of persons carrying out that mission a *congregation*!

Again, you and your church cannot opt out of the mission of making disciples. Making disciples is what churches do. A church that is not about disciple making is not a church. It may be a social club or a family group, perhaps, but it is not a church; for what churches do is make disciples. To be a church is to be about the mission of making disciples. That's a functional definition of a church.

Now, what about your church? Is it about making disciples? Is the congregation that gathers weekly in the building you call your church actively engaged in making disciples? Are the folks who make up your congregation disciples themselves?

That's what this workbook is all about. It matters not at all if your congregation consists of four to six people gathered to worship every other Sunday morning or if your congregation consists of three thousand people gathering in five services of worship every Sunday. The questions are the same:

- What is a disciple?

- Are we in this church here and now disciples?

- Are we as a congregation about the mission of making disciples?

- How can we be even more intentional about our mission of making disciples?

- How can we involve everyone in our entire congregation in the mission of making disciples?

- How can we steadily and constantly grow in our mission of making disciples? (And a practical issue: How can we measure our growth and progress in our disciple-making mission?)

That's what this workbook is all about. It's about the mission of your congregation. And that mission is to make disciples of Jesus Christ.

## Getting Started

Remember this is not a book to be read alone!

As we said in the introduction, this is a workbook, to be read, discussed, and used by many persons in your congregation at the same time. Reading this book in isolation may be interesting, but it will accomplish little. This book is designed and intended to be used as a workbook by a group of persons in your congregation who have caught the idea that they must be about disciple-making and who want to get serious about doing so. So gather the groups and work through this book together.

To develop a disciple-formation process that is unique to your church's context, each step of this process needs a foundation of prayer. Keep the prayer strategy moving forward. If you have identified a prayer team to undergird this effort, make sure they stay informed about the specifics for prayer. At this step, they can be praying for the Holy Spirit to guide and direct the identification of the people needed to make this disciple-formation process happen.

You will want to pay special attention to how the group works together. As you begin to think about how to develop a disciple-formation process for your local church, you might consider as a first step the question, "Whom should we appoint to this committee?" Often the candidates are people who are already in leadership roles in church life and who don't really need one more thing to do. Sometimes we choose people who don't have the needed gifts, skills, and visioning ability that this type of work requires. As we have stated, your beginning team may already be chosen. You might begin with a staff team, an Administrative Council, or a Council on Ministries.

But rather than leaping to the appointment of a committee or relying only on existing groups, you might think about putting together a new group of six to twelve people, including the pastor. The purpose of this group is to plan and implement, over the course of nine months, an intentional, disciple-formation process for your church. You will want to invite people who are grounded in the spiritual practices of prayer, Scripture study, worship, small group involvement (your church can interpret this in whatever way is appropriate for your context), and a ministry involvement (your church can interpret this in whatever way is appropriate for your context). This group will be different from a committee because they will have one focus, because they will have a beginning and ending point for working together (to be determined by the team and your church), and because they don't fall under any prescribed format for United Methodist committees as detailed in *The Book of Discipline*. The On Developing a Team section provides helps for your teamwork together.

You and the group might want to devote the first session of your time together to getting acquainted, outlining the whole purpose and process of this group endeavor, and focusing on that first chapter in some detail. Make sure everyone understands the mission of the Church—but just not in the abstract. That means everyone needs to understand that making disciples is the mission and purpose of your congregation, of the congregation of folks you've gathered together to consider this process. "The mission of the church is *our* mission!"

The workbook is like a roadmap or a nautical chart. You need to study it thoroughly before you start out on your journey by land or by sea. But studying the map or chart is not the journey. The journey itself is undertaken after the chart is studied, then laid aside. And the journey will take far longer than you devote to studying the map. This workbook is the chart or map; you and your congregation will embark on an exciting journey after studying it. That journey may take a year, several years, or many years as your congregation commits itself to growing as a congregation that is about the mission of the church.

What's that mission again? Right! The mission of the church is to make disciples of Jesus Christ!

## Role of the Team

The team needs to take the lead on this Bible study, bringing it to the congregation in whatever ways are appropriate for your context. The team can strategize about communication with the congregation. This strategizing should be done in coordination with the pastor,

## Role of the Pastor

It is always good to take advantage of opportunities to preach on the mission of your church to motivate, inspire, and stir people. This shouldn't be seen as a "once a year, whether they need it or not" type of sermon. Preach the mission strategically. The pastor also needs to be casting a vision for disciple formation through sermons, newsletter, teaching opportunities – any means to get the message out of what it can look like for the church to develop a disciple formation process that is unique to your context.

## Role of the Congregation

The congregation should be challenged to find a way to engage in the Bible study. Let the congregation members suggest ways to participate, if the planned opportunities are not accessible to all.

## Check the Emotional Climate

When churches begin to talk about mission, someone might begin to get anxious. As the leadership and the congregation begin to align around the mission, fear, apathy, and/or cynicism can begin to develop. This is normal. Be alert to the emotional climate at this stage. Invite the person on the Team who is gifted for this to be in conversation with various members of the congregation, test the waters, take the temperature of the congregation, and see how people are feeling.

## Going Deeper

Have the team review "Baptismal Covenant I" in the *United Methodist Hymnal*. Have the group discuss the meaning of the historic questions in regard to our baptismal commitment to mission.

## Before Moving On

- The final decision of who makes up this team should be made. The team should meet together as often as necessary, and become united, as described above.

- All team members should be committed to the concept that the most important role for your congregation is to make disciples for Jesus Christ. Everything you do should contribute in some way to that mission.

- The team should have developed a list of ideas on ways to help the entire congregation have this same commitment, and begin to make decisions on how to implement these ideas.

- Capture all ideas on newsprint and have someone record them for future reference.

(Handout)

## CHAPTER 1 BIBLE STUDY

# BIBLE STUDY: OUR MISSION

This study can take one to three sessions and can be used in a number of ways:

1.) Sunday school classes and small groups could work through the study together.

2.) The pastor and/or disciple-formation team members could lead specially scheduled weekly sessions

3.) The pastor could preach a sermon series on the themes of the Bible study (other texts around the theme of discipleship: Micah 6:8, Galatians 5:22-23, Nicodemus, the woman at the well, Peter, Saul/Paul, etc.).

4.) Your team may come up with another idea.

Open with prayer. Read Matthew 28:16-20.

Reflect and record on paper: What do you think of when you hear these words in verse 19, "Go and make disciples of all nations"?

Relate in discussion: Have you ever been involved in making a new disciple of Jesus Christ? What was your part in that process? What was the part of the Holy Spirit in that process?

We might think that we've never been involved in making a new disciple. But if we think carefully we might recall:

- teaching a child or youth Sunday school class

- talking with someone who was in a crisis of faith

- doing a loving work for an unknown person

- sharing part of our faith story with someone else

Spend some time talking about how a person grows as a disciple. Identify some of the things that can lead a person to grow closer to Christ.

Have someone read aloud Matthew 22:37-40.

Reflect and Record on paper: How do you practice love of God and neighbor in your daily life?

Relate in discussion: Do you grow deeper in love of God and neighbor as you mature in your faith? Can you name ways that you've grown deeper? What are specific things that have helped you grow deeper along the way (individuals, ministries of your church, etc.)? How is growing deeper in love of God and neighbor related to the process of discipleship?

John and Charles Wesley, the founders of the Methodist movement, believed that growing deeper (more perfect) in love of God and neighbor was the purpose of a discipleship process. But it is a life long journey.

Have someone read aloud Matthew 28:16-20 and Matthew 22:37-40.

Reflect and Record on paper: What is the link between these two passages? How do they connect or relate to one another?

Have copies of paragraphs 120, 121, & 122 of *The Book of Discipline of the United Methodist Church 2004*, available for each person. Distribute the copies and allow people time to read.

Relate in discussion: Do you agree with paragraph 120, as it identifies the mission for the Church? Is the local church the most significant arena through which disciple making occurs? Why or why not?

- If your church's mission is paragraph 120, spend some time talking about how your church is living out of this mission. Does everything you do as a church focus on and support the mission of making disciples?

- If your church has a specific different mission statement, distribute it now, and invite discussion about whether it is in alignment with paragraph 120. The goal for this discussion is to discover points of connection with the "making disciples" mission statement. Is your mission allowing a context for making disciples? If not, is there a way to make that happen, so that your church can better live out of the mission to make disciples?

Do you agree with paragraph 121, as it provides a rationale for the mission of making disciples in the context of the two Matthew passages?

Paragraph 122 describes that discipleship process as "proclaim, seek, welcome, gather, lead, nurture, and send." The General Board of Discipleship has described that process as "inviting, welcoming, nurturing, and sending."

A disciple-formation process helps a person move from one level of discipleship to the next to the next, growing deeper as a disciple of Jesus Christ, and growing deeper in love of God and neighbor.

Close in prayer, in whatever way seems appropriate.

# On Developing a Team

## *Assumptions about the Team*

Whether you begin with an existing group or a new task group, the Team you are building for your church has one purpose: the development of a disciple-formation process that is unique to your church's context.

Your team should have a maximum of twelve persons, including the pastor. This size will allow for efficiency in decision making, accountability, and care for one another.

There should be one person on the Team who is responsible for watching the emotional climate of the Team (taking the emotional temperature of the Team on a regular basis).

Your team may divide into sub-teams, which may in turn build teams for accomplishing a specific task, function, or sub-purpose. There needs to be an intentional system for individual sub-teams to be connected and communicate; generally that will happen through the Team leadership.

Your team will be engaging in discernment about the development of the disciple-formation process, inviting the congregation to be seeking discernment with the Team.

Your team will be developing a plan for communication with the congregation throughout the implementation of this plan, as a means of continuing to build buy-in.

## Getting Started on Building a Team

To get started, initiate a discussion with those on the team. Discuss together the following:

1. People often have misconceptions about teams. How do you respond to these misconceptions?

- Teams are sluggish and hard to steer

- Micromanagement is normal and good

- On a team everyone has to do the same thing

What other misconceptions can you think of?

2. There are different types of teams. Some teams are short-term, or tactical. Others are long-term, or strategic. Is this a short-term or long-term team you're forming?

3. First Corinthians 12 contains biblical imagery characterizing the church as a body.

How important are the following qualities/characteristics of the body?

- Trust

- Ability to make decisions together

- Small group vulnerability

- All are needed and important

- Noticeable personal growth

- Ability to learn and evaluate together

What other qualities or characteristics would you add?

## Relational Team Building

After a team has been formed, the members need to spend time together building relationships before moving directly to the task. There are many tools and resources available for building a sense of group life. One example is for each person to spend time sharing about an important time, event, place, etc. in their life where faith was formed. Leadership should take time to adequately accomplish this in the first meeting.

It might be helpful at this point to have the entire Team go through a Bible study on 1 Corinthians 12. Study and meditation on Scripture will continue to play a key role in working through this guide. Establish this practice from the beginning of your work together.

## Working Together

Set regular times for your team to meet. Expect it to take a few times for members to establish the calendar. Leadership may need to help people say "no" to other church activities, in order to give attention to the development of your disciple-formation process.

It could be useful for the team to examine your church's current practices regarding how and why decisions are made. What drives decisions? Is it money, past practice, or something else? What changes could be or might be needed and implemented?

It will be helpful for the team to be informed about the nature of change in organizations. Much has been written about change and paradigm shifts, both from a secular and religious perspective. One secular resource is *Leading Change,* by John Kotter, published by the Harvard Business School Press (Boston: 1996). Give particular attention to his "Eight Stages of Change."

# WHAT'S A DISCIPLE?

The goal of this chapter is to discover and express a definition of the word "disciple," including a list of spiritual practices of a disciple, which will be unique to the context of your local church.

## Centering Prayer

*God of unity and love, we thank you for your guidance during this process. As we work to gain a common understanding of a disciple, and as we seek to define spiritual practices, keep us focused on you. May you unite this congregation so that we may embrace for ourselves who you call us to be. We pray in the name of Christ, who unites us in one body. Amen.*

## Chapter at a Glance

### GOALS

- Discover the definition of a disciple

- Define the spiritual practices of a disciple

- Find ways to unify the team and congregation on this definition

- Begin to discover how your congregation can fulfill the mission of the Church, which is to make disciples for Jesus Christ

## TIMEFRAME SUGGESTIONS

It may take multiple sessions to cover the material in this chapter. You will need ample time together for search and discovery activities and Bible study.

## POSSIBLE FORMAT

- Read the centering prayer together, or have the facilitator read while the group meditates.

- Have Bibles, or copies of Matthew 28:16-20 available for everyone.

- Read the passage aloud, inviting participants to follow along. Ask the group the following three questions: (Capture answers on newsprint)

  - How would you define a disciple of Jesus Christ?

  - Do you see yourself as being one? Why or why not?

  - What are the basic practices that you do as a disciple?

- Defining Activity: Facilitator asks the team to define "disciple" in as many ways as they can. They should do this in total silence. Ask each person to jot down words or short phrases that describe "disciple" on sticky notes, then to place these sticky notes on a wall under a sentence stem like "A disciple of Jesus Christ is a person who . . ." This should take several minutes. When finished, ask one person to read all the sticky notes aloud, while the rest of the group members cluster these notes into rough categories. Some of the categories might be "beliefs," another "actions," another "relationships," another "expectations," etc.

  - *A hint for the facilitator, which you may want to share with the team: Watch out for "tautologies." A "tautology" is a sentence that defines a word "in a circle." In other words, it simply gives another name for the word being defined without really defining it. Example: In a recent conversation, a young man was asked to define "evil." He replied that "evil" was doing sinful things. When asked what sinful acts were, he said that sinful acts were things that were evil. A circle? That's why what we call functional definitions are more useful. Ask the team to think about a person they consider a disciple and list words that describe the person, rather than focusing on a dictionary definition of a disciple.*

- From the headings and words underneath, have the team develop their own sentence defining a disciple.

- There will need to be an ongoing spirit of discernment among team members as you go through this process.

- You need to always be asking yourselves if what you're seeing is in keeping with our biblical and Wesleyan theology.

- Working together as a team, begin to construct a one sentence definition of disciple.

- Start with "A disciple is . . ." Test your definition against your mission statement, against Matthew 28:19-20, and against our Wesleyan theology (a good source for understanding John Wesley's definition of "disciple" is his sermon "A More Excellent Way").

- Work with your material until everyone on the team can stand in consensus with the definition.

- Close in prayer, in whatever way is appropriate.

## Individual Preparation

What's the mission of the Church again? Yes, you've heard it over and over again. But once more:

**The mission of the congregation is to make disciples of Jesus Christ.**

So what is a disciple?

If the Church is supposed to make disciples, then just what is a disciple?

A first thought might be turning to the Great Commission, Matthew 28:16-20. In this, the risen Christ tells the twelve apostles to go into the world to make disciples. But that doesn't tell us what a disciple is.

Let's put this idea another way: If our job is to make disciples, how do we know when we've accomplished that task? How do we know if we've "made" a disciple? What does a disciple look like? Act like? What does a disciple do that is different from what everyone else does? And do we make a disciple like we make a cake or a birdhouse? "There. It's finished. Now let's do something else." (Another way of saying that: "Once a disciple, always a disciple." True? Let's think about that one.)

The place to start, of course, is with the Scriptures. The Bible gives us clues and insights that we want to plumb in order to understand as profoundly as possible just what a disciple is. But simply reading about the disciples—or the apostles—in the New Testament doesn't give us a full understanding of what a disciple is today.

(Let's clear up a bit of technical language here. Jesus chose twelve persons to be apostles. The term *apostles* refers to these twelve—even though the lists of the names of these twelve are not the same in all the versions of the gospel. See Matthew 10:1-4; Mark 3:13-19a; and Luke 6:12-16. But before each of these twelve was selected as an apostle, that person was a disciple. In other words, an apostle is not a different order or level of disciple. The word *apostle* simply refers to the twelve who formed what some scholars have called the immediate and intimate group around Jesus throughout his ministry. So what we are describing in this chapter are not the twelve apostles; we're talking about disciples.)

According to the gospels, Jesus had many disciples. These included men and women, young people and old, children and youth, Jews and Gentiles, rich and poor, city dwellers and country folk, the very religious and the slightly religious. What bound them together, what made them as one, was their allegiance to Jesus.

Let's put that another way: Perhaps the only common characteristic that all the disciples of Jesus shared was that they all believed in Jesus (at least, most of the time), in what he was doing, and in what he was teaching as he roamed the Holy Land. Yes, they all lived in one geographic area and at one period of history, but these characteristics are not too significant for our discussion. All those disciples of Jesus *believed* in what Jesus was teaching, but like you and me, not all of them *understood* all that Jesus was teaching. But, again like you and me, all were struck by the winsomeness of his words and all were anxious to see what he would say and do next.

Are you getting any clues yet as to what a disciple of Jesus Christ is? Let's list some possible insights in a short-hand way. You can change, adapt, modify, adjust, or even reject these based on your own understanding.

A person who is a disciple of Jesus Christ is a person who:

- Recognizes that Jesus is someone very special and unique, someone out of the ordinary, someone who is "charismatic" in the very best sense of the word.

- Chooses to follow Jesus Christ. This person chooses to follow because of the power and presence of Jesus Christ. This person is not forced or compelled to follow. This person follows because she or he decides or her on his own to do so.

- Believes that Jesus Christ offers the way not only to life eternal but, also important, to life abundant. That way may not be immediately clear and obvious, but the disciple believes that Jesus Christ is revealing that way.

- Commits himself or herself to Jesus Christ. What does that mean? That means that that person has consciously decided to put Jesus Christ—who Christ is, what Christ does, and what Christ teaches—at the center or her or his life. Christ becomes the lens through which that person views the world and all the people in it.

- Entrusts herself or himself entirely to Jesus Christ. Such a person clings to Jesus Christ as a drowning individual clings to a bit of driftwood—as that person's only hope.

- May not understand all that Jesus Christ is teaching and doing, but is willing to follow and to grow in understanding and insight. Such a person may be content with the fact that she or he may never understand completely all that Jesus Christ means, but that's all right. He or she understands enough to follow Jesus Christ completely.

- Lives a life that reflects her or his belief and trust in Jesus the Christ. That life is marked by action, by doing, not just by believing or saying. Remember what the Epistles of James has to say on this score (and if you don't remember, stop right now and read James 1:22-27; 2:14-26).

Now—and this is very important—*you* add some more characteristics of a disciple. Do not be content with this list. This list is a beginning list; it's a list intended to "prime the pump," to get you (and the members of your group) thinking. It is certainly not an exhaustive list; it is an illustrative list. The most important characteristics are the characteristics you add.

A couple of comments as you and your group members add to this list.

Nowhere in this list is a comment about what is sometimes called "being saved" or "giving your heart to Jesus." This is not to disparage these concepts; they are rich in tradition and based in Scripture. But you and I cannot define for someone else how she or he will make a commitment to follow Jesus Christ. That commitment may come in a blinding flash, as it did to Paul on the road to Damascus. It may come slowly over time, as it did to the apostles Thomas and Peter. It may come in "fits and starts" as it did to John Wesley, one of the founders of what we know as the Methodist movement.

You see, because each of us is an individual, we will respond to Jesus Christ in our own individual ways. We cannot evaluate another's decision to follow Jesus, especially if we evaluate it alongside our decision to follow Jesus. The gospels are rich in stories of how different persons responded to Jesus, but each responded in his or her own unique way.

And second, just as we cannot dictate how another will make a commitment to Jesus Christ, neither can we dictate the form or the living out of that commitment. What's that mean? Simply this: Disciples of Jesus Christ are called by Christ to undertake a bewildering variety of tasks. No one task is more "disciple-like" than another. God does not call all disciples to be choir members or Sunday School teachers or preachers or trustees or any other one or two things. God *does* call all disciples to a careful and prayerful discernment—that means discovery —of God's call on their lives through Jesus Christ. What's the upshot of all of this? Your neighbor is not less a disciple of Jesus Christ than you are just because he or she does not live out his or her discipleship the same way you do! The common denominator is that all disciples do what they do out of a commitment to Jesus Christ.

All of the time? Of course not. Disciples stumble and fall (remember that old Methodist word "backslide"?) but disciples experience forgiveness through the grace of God, so they pick themselves up, dust themselves off, and begin again to live as forgiven people. And to live as a forgiven person is to respond to God's grace by actively loving that which God loves. What is that? "That" is our sisters and brothers next door and around the world. We love because God first loved us through Christ.

Shorthand? Disciples are people who demonstrate their love of and response to Christ by loving one another in word, in deed, in prayer, and in every other possible way. Want to add something like that to your list of characteristics of a disciple?

Wow! This only makes the mission of disciple-making more difficult, doesn't it? It might be easier if we could say all disciples experience a call to discipleship in this way or that way and all disciples do this or that in response to that call. But that simply is not the case. This may make our task of making disciples a bit more difficult, but the results will be infinitely richer for it!

## Role of the Team

Your role is to lead the process of developing a "church owned" definition of a disciple, including a list of spiritual practices of a disciple. As your definition is being developed, ask for input from your congregation on what they think is the definition of a disciple. Write down the agreed upon definition of a disciple and put it in a place where you can see it daily. Ask God to show you every day the ways you need to grow as a disciple. In this way, your congregation will begin to build ownership of the definition.

Find additional ways to share with other members of the congregation what you're learning about the definition of a disciple. As appropriate, include this conversation in small groups that you're a part of.

## Role of the Pastor

The role of the pastor, as spiritual leader of the congregation, is to be fully engaged in the development and sharing of the definition of a disciple. This definition can be shared in sermons, newsletters, Christian conferencing, and other communication venues normally used in your congregation.

## Role of the Congregation

The congregation, or representative group(s) of the congregation, has a clear role to be giving input into the development of the definition of a disciple and the list of spiritual practices. To that end, this group(s) of people needs to be listening to God, to one another, and be in conversation with the Team to achieve this end.

## Check the Emotional Climate

There are likely to be differences of opinion and interpretation along the way in this part of the process. The reason for developing a "church-owned" definition of a disciple is precisely because there are differences of opinion about what a disciple is among people in churches. The person on the Team who is charged with being aware of the emotional climate will need to keep eyes, ears, and heart tuned to what people are saying behind closed doors. Keep communication lines very open and clear. Once again, say things many times, in many different ways.

## Going Deeper

Some people who have been Christians for a long time will say, "Everybody knows what a disciple is! We don't need to define it!" But much that goes on in our churches does not flow out of a desire for disciple making. If we understand our mission to be about making disciples, we need to be clear what a disciple is. The task of creating a common definition of *disciple* for your congregation can be a helpful, informative, and inspiring work. As the congregation begins to gain consensus around a definition of disciple, it will help them understand more clearly what the church is trying to "produce" as the congregation fulfills the mission to make disciples.

On their own time, have group members consider:

- How would you define a disciple of Jesus Christ?

- Do you see yourself as being one? Why or why not?

- What are the basic practices that you do as a disciple?

Other passages to consider:

Matthew 8:5-13 (the story of the centurion, a man who had absolute confidence in the authority of Jesus)

Acts 9:19b-22 (the story of Saul, whose mission was redefined by Christ)

Acts 8:26-39 (the story of the Ethiopian Eunuch, who eagerly desired to be baptized that he might be identified as a disciple)

Matthew 9:35–10:8 (the story of Jesus asking the disciples to pray for workers, then sending them out to be the workers)

John 4:1-30 (the woman at the well)

Acts 20:1-6 (part of the story of Paul's missionary travels)

Acts 2:14-42 (Peter's powerful sermon on the day of Pentecost, and the subsequent addition of 3,000 persons into the faith)

John 9 (the story of the man born blind, who was healed by Jesus)

Philippians 2 (having the mind of Christ in humility)

## Additional Resources

For help with spiritual practices, *Way to Live*, ed. by Dorothy C. Bass & Don C. Richter; (Nashville: Upper Room Books, 2002).

For a different way of approaching Bible study, *Listening to God*, by John Ackerman; (The Alban Institute, 2001), exercise 3, page 130.

For some definitions of basic Christian terms from a Wesleyan perspective, see *A Faithful Future, vol. 2*, (Nashville: Discipleship Resources, 2003) "Learning the Terms" on page 53.

Brian McLaren's Bible study on disciple-making in *More Ready Than You Realize* (Grand Rapids: Zondervan, 2002) focuses on seven qualities of a disciple, p 160.

## Before Moving On

The team should be able to articulate the definition and spiritual practices of a disciple

Team members should be committed themselves to living out the life of a disciple

Specific ideas should be generated, and implemented where appropriate throughout your congregation, on ways to develop a common understanding, definition, and desire to live as a disciple

Beginning thoughts should be listed as to how your congregation is currently and/or could be fulfilling the mission of making disciples for Jesus Christ

# LOOKING AROUND

As one of the steps in determining a particular disciple-formation process for your congregation, it will be helpful for you to look at several examples of disciple forming processes (historical and current). You will also need to keep in mind the necessary components required for a healthy disciple-formation process.

## Centering Prayer

*Holy and wondrous God, you were present and active in the world since the beginning of time, and we have much to learn from your activity throughout the span of life. As we learn, work, and grow together, teach us how we can learn from the faithful who have gone before us, and teach us how to learn from those who are making disciples now. May the principles that guided them guide us as we seek to make disciples; and in all things, God, keep our eyes focused on the teachings and actions of Jesus, in whose name we pray. Amen.*

## Chapter at a Glance

### GOALS

- To become familiar with what a disciple-formation process looks like.

- To study and understand John Wesley's disciple-formation process.

- To examine some examples of disciple-formation systems that other churches use.

- To understand the various typical stages of disciple formation.

- To understand the means of grace.

- To develop a list of essential components to have as part of your church's disciple-formation process.

## TIMEFRAME SUGGESTIONS

This chapter may take multiple sessions to complete. You might consider one session just for the purpose of reviewing John Wesley's disciple-formation system.

## POSSIBLE FORMAT

- Read the centering prayer together, or have the facilitator read while the group meditates

- Review *Bible Study: Fullness of the Word* together

- Discuss Wesley's disciple-formation processes, as well as the processes from other congregations. As you review the processes, consider the following questions (and capture information on newsprint):

  - How might the system carry out the church's mission and help lead the congregation toward attaining God's vision?

  - How does the system offer various entry points into the process, since persons become part of a church at various points on their faith journey?

  - How does the system focus on the faith journey of individuals and the congregation as a whole? Does it focus on lifelong formation, rather than programs that provide quick fixes?

  - How does the system include faith-forming ministries for all ages, including children and youth?

  - How does the process acknowledge the fact that human beings develop their faith at different rates, levels, or stages as being important to a successful disciple-formation process? (See *Understanding Levels and Stages* under Additional Resources.)

- How does the process incorporate some aspect of our Wesleyan heritage (kinds of grace, practicing the means of grace, acts of piety/mercy, following the General Rules, etc.)? (See studies on Wesley in Additional Resources.)

- How does the process provide guidelines for those engaged in the system? How are practices of faith, means of grace, and the church-owned definition of disciple the developing guidelines for what it means to grow in faith?

- What identified resources in the process help individuals move from stage to stage, increasing the flow of intentional growth?

- What image or metaphor for discipleship emerges from this process?

- How is the process relevant to your congregational context?

• What new principles have emerged from examining the various systems, both Wesley's and current church processes? Make a list of the principles you want to make sure are a part of your congregation's disciple-formation process.

## Individual Preparation

Okay. What's the mission of the Church again? To make disciples of Jesus Christ. So how does a congregation focus its energies toward that mission? You gotta wanna. Historically the church has created systems and processes to meet the needs of the moment in their efforts to make disciples. What makes those processes effective in the mission? Well, they follow certain principles. We will soon have a chance to look at your own setting to assess how you're doing in disciple making. But first we'll look at some processes already in place and see what principles we can learn about how to effectively make disciples.

Discipleship is a process. The apostle John (John 1:16) tells us that we receive grace upon grace, which John Wesley felt reflected a process. Discipleship requires forward movement. Understanding faith as a continuous journey can be a daunting task for some people. Congregations are made up of people who are on this journey together, but are at different levels of faith formation. Therefore, it is important that you develop a set of markers or stages for the journey. Such markers allow people associated with your congregation to see personal growth, as well as a goal toward which they can work.

At this point, we will peruse both historical and current disciple-formation processes. As we review them, we will look for principles of disciple-formation processes. If the congregation looks only at the processes themselves, and not at the principles that shape the processes, the Team will have a temptation to borrow the entire process. Remember your local context. Wesley's disciple-forming process has general principles that can help you in your local congregation, but his entire process will not work in a local church. The same is true for contemporary examples—Willow Creek, Saddleback, Brentwood UMC, Christ/Riverside UMC's and others; seek to glean their overarching principles, and not their programs.

## Wesley's Disciple-Forming Process

John Wesley believed that Christians journey on a path toward human perfection—the way of salvation. The path toward perfection is marked by various types of grace. Prevenient grace is given to all persons, and works in their lives before they encounter Christ. At some point, prevenient grace moves people enough to be convicted of their sins, a gift called convincing grace. When people are moved to repent of their sins, they receive justifying grace, assuring them of God's presence in their lives and giving them new life in Christ. Sanctifying grace moves people onward toward Christian perfection. Such movement of grace reminds us that Wesley believed Christians are on a spiritual pilgrimage. For Wesley, the movement of grace upon grace is evidenced by continual growth in love of God and neighbor.

In order to facilitate continual growth in persons seeking to grow deeper as disciples, Wesley organized the people called Methodists into groups for public service. As people experienced God through those service encounters, they moved into trial bands. If they were growing as a result of their experiences in a trial band, they became members in a united society (large group, or church). Each person in the united society also belonged to a smaller group, called a class, which was located in the person's neighborhood. Some moved into bands, which were voluntary, smaller groups that met for confession, prayer, and spiritual growth. Through fellowship and Christian conversation, bands gained mutual accountability, nurture and growth in grace. Wesley's process allowed people to move through stages of growth and development toward spiritual maturity—always growing deeper in their love of God and neighbor.

## Current Disciple-Formation Processes

Today some well-known large churches such as Saddleback, Willow Creek, and Ginghamsburg have processes in place, and you can look at their published resources to find out more information about the processes that work in their particular context. As you look toward current disciple formation processes, remember to look for their principles, and not programs. Look also beyond the scope of your context to non-western processes, multicultural processes, and even beyond the context of the church to addiction recovery models and twelve-step models. The following United Methodist examples will help get you started in studying current disciple-formation processes. The purpose of studying those already-in-place processes is to learn principles that you will want to apply to your own context.

**Christ United Methodist Church (CUMC) in East Moline, IL; Riverside United Methodist Church (RUMC) in Moline, IL; and ChaingLink Student Ministry in Moline, IL**. CUMC, RUMC, and ChaingLink have worked together for several years in the area of discipleship and youth ministry. Together, they developed a church-owned definition of disciple, and defined spiritual practices that faithful followers of Jesus Christ engage in: prayer, outreach, worship, evangelizing, relationship, use of gifts, and Scripture. Those practices form an acronym, POWER US, which the congregations use as a means of accountability and growth. In small groups, classes, team meetings, and other group gatherings, members ask one another to give examples of how they grow in their practices. People visit the website www.powerus.org to discern where they are in each practice. The cooperative ministry offers both individual and congregational opportunities for each person to grow deeper in these practices of faith. Children, youth, and adults all engage in these varied opportunities.

**Brentwood United Methodist Church in Brentwood, TN**. Brentwood UMC seeks to engage people in a lifelong process of discipleship, using river imagery as a means to mark points along a spiritual journey. Persons are invited to go through a discernment process for five weeks, focusing on a different river marker each week. Each week focuses on a Scripture for reflection, questions for further reflection, and a guide to prayer. Once a person determines where they are in the river of life, s/he is invited to be involved in workshops, classes, and various ministry opportunities that move them further on the journey. Brentwood UMC also offers different opportunities for children and youth to engage movement from marker to marker.

**St. Luke's United Methodist Church in Orlando, FL.** St. Luke's UMC uses a ministry matrix to offer opportunities for spiritual growth. The spiritual formation ministry team and small group ministry group provide five categories, or stages, of Christian faith. They focus on how to reach persons in each stage through invitation, and make decisions about opportunities based on a movement from stage to stage. The teams provide the congregation with a variety of opportunities for growth, knowing that each person's journey is unique.

**Bethany United Methodist Church in Austin, TX.** Bethany UMC engages Scripture as a means to promote holistic growth, based on the Great Commandment. (See Mark 12:28-34) Bethany's process is expressed in the form of a circle divided into four quadrants—heart, mind, soul, and strength. The circle contains a series of concentric circles, and various ministries are listed in each concentric circle and quadrant. (See p. 89 for a similar diagram.) Congregants are invited to use the circle as a self-assessment, marking those ministries in which they are involved. Bethany UMC hopes that each person engages in growth and ministry opportunities that move them toward the center of the circle, ever-focusing on Jesus Christ.

These are just examples of churches that understand that people move through different stages as they grow deeper in discipleship. Your church can do the same!

## The Role of the Team

The team needs to be open to learning about healthy disciple-formation processes—both historical and current processes. They will want to include Wesley's process and current processes in the United Methodist Church, but will also want to look beyond to other historic processes and current cultural processes.

## The Role of the Pastor

The pastor needs to cast the vision of what a disciple-forming process means for the congregation. S/he needs to teach the congregation, especially about Wesley's system and how it works in today's context. S/he also needs to support the work of the Team as they engage in study and dialogue with the congregation (and each other).

## The Role of the Congregation

The congregation needs to provide input throughout this section. The congregation may engage in the suggested Bible studies, or they may want to try some of the current Wesleyan processes. The congregation needs to be informed throughout the development process. Continue to test the Team's work with them to make sure it is understood and embraced.

## Check the Emotional Climate

Some people may not understand the need for process. In fact, they may not understand the concept of a process, so your discerned rationale behind the "need" and "concept" should be clearly communicated and explained in a variety of ways. Help people understand why these two terms are important.

As you study the various examples included above, some may resist them, saying things like, "We're not Saddleback," or "Wesley's dead, so why is that pertinent now?" It will help the Team and the congregation understand that they study the examples, not to use the examples themselves, but to use the *principles* the examples are built upon in order to create their own, unique processes for their context.

Similarly, as you study examples, there may be a tendency to "cut and paste" from the examples to form your own process. The examples have each been built on principles, and are unique to the ministry setting in which they are used. Congregations cannot expect that portions of someone else's process will work for them, simply because it has been a successful process somewhere else. A constant reminder and checking of the local context will help.

As the team, pastor, and congregation study these examples, they may struggle with making a connection to the processes they study. "What does this have to do with us?" may be a question that arises as you study. The team and pastor need to continue building connections for each other and for the congregation as they seek to learn the principles that guide disciple-formation processes, and as they discover the key components to healthy processes.

# Going Deeper

### *Other Historical Disciple-Formation Processes*

*The Spiritual Exercises of St. Ignatius*: Ignatius was born in 1491 and died in 1556. He began his spiritual journey in 1521, and after careful study and meditation, began to write his *Spiritual Exercises* in 1522. His exercises are set in a weekly rhythm, and include study, prayer, and reflection. The *Exercises* intend to move believers closer to God with each self-examination. Many editions are available. Louis Puhl's translation (New York: Vintage Spiritual Classics (division of Random House), 2000) has both an easy layout and simple language for comprehension.

The *Rule* of St. Benedict: St. Benedict wrote his *Rule* as a way to provide uniformity of Christian practice during the late fifth or early sixth century. The seventy-three chapters of the *Rule* seek to lead a Christian toward God, and are intended for beginners in the spiritual life. Topics include community, silence, humility, prayer, care for the old and sick, spiritual reading, and charity. Many chapters relate the ordering of a monastery, but the practices of Christian faith may be helpful in discerning stages or faith practices for your congregation's disciple formation process.

You may also want to review historical catechisms, such as Luther's short catechism, as a way to grasp disciple-formation processes.

## Understand Levels and Stages

How you develop stages for your own process is entirely up to you. The various stages need to be born out of your church's mission, the vision for disciple formation, the community (which is why context is important—these are the people you are trying to reach), and your church-owned definition of a disciple. Therefore, your stages may be for individuals, or it may arise out of United Methodist Church's core process (inviting, welcoming, nurturing, and sending) of the congregation. As you develop these stages, a description of what a person looks like at that stage may be helpful. It might be helpful if you continue working to develop a metaphor or image that speaks to your congregation, because your stages can relate to the metaphor.

You may also want to refer to the article "Creating a Discipleship System for Youth and Young Adults," found in *Making God Real for a New Generation*, by Craig Kennet Miller and MaryJane Pierce Norton (Nashville: Discipleship Resources, 2003). Page 130 suggests stages of discipleship: cautious, curious, committed, professing, and inviting.

Other examples of stages in use are:

*Christ UMC, Riverside UMC, and ChaingLink:* Chaos, Community, Connection, Covenant, and Coaching.

*Brentwood UMC*: Checking out the Scene, Stepping in the Water, Diving Deeper, Riding the Rapids, and Going Fishing.

*St. Luke's UMC*: One-Hour Christians, Seeker Christians, Growing Christians, Maturing Christians, and Core Ministry Christians.

*Bethany UMC*: No "stages" are identified through words, but through the concentric circles, moving people closer and close to the center of the circle, which is Christ.

## Additional Resources

James Fowler's six stages of faith may be helpful for you. An Internet query will point you toward numerous websites that contain descriptions of those stages.

If you want to find out more information about Wesley's disciple-formation process, here are some resources your congregation can study:

Clapper, Gregory S. *As if the Heart Mattered.* Nashville: Upper Room Books, 1997. Clapper's book offers Biblical and theological reflections on spirituality. Each chapter also includes insights into Wesleyan spirituality, the sermons and hymns of the Wesleys, and questions for reflection and discussion.

Harper, Steve. *Devotional Life in the Wesleyan Tradition.* This manual, for use in small groups, gives persons time for daily reflection upon John Wesley and how his spiritual practices can apply to the modern individual and congregation.

Manskar, Steven W. *Accountable Discipleship.* Nashville: Discipleship Resources, 2000. Manskar lays out the basic tenants of Wesleyan theology in practical ways. Chapters 3 and 4 are particularly helpful in fleshing out more of Wesley's framework on discipleship.

Stookey, Laurence Hull. *This Day: A Wesleyan Way of Prayer.* Nashville: Abingdon Press, 2004. This book guides individuals in devotional life throughout the year, aiding them in Scripture reading and prayer. The accompanying books by Denise Stringer (*How Is It With Your Soul?*) aid congregations in forming modern band meetings for the spiritual formation of the society or modern congregation.

## Before Moving On

- Develop a list of essential components to have as part of your church's disciple-formation process, and have copies ready for individual team members.

- Please note there is an optional exercise in chapter 4 that requires the bringing together of a group. If you choose to do this exercise, you'll need to prepare a group in advance. See p. 52 for details

(Handout)

## CHAPTER 3 BIBLE STUDY

# FULLNESS OF THE WORD

Engage the Team in a Bible study on John 1:14-16. The following questions may guide reflection on the passage.

1. The fullness of the Word is Christ's glory when he became flesh. What does it mean to you that Christ became flesh and lived on earth?

2. We are recipients of the word's fullness. How do you recognize the movement of the Word in your life? In the life of the congregation?

3. The fullness we receive is grace, which occurs in abundance and great frequency. How have you experienced "grace upon grace," and how has it affected you? Where have you seen the congregation experience it, and what has been the effect of grace on the congregation?

4. "Grace upon grace" implies continual growth. How does the image of us receiving "grace upon grace" relate to disciple formation?

# WHAT ARE WE DOING?

In this chapter we will examine ways to assess the current reality of disciple making in your congregation. We will introduce examples of tools you might use to identify the components of your current process.

## Centering Prayer

*Ever-faithful God, we thank you for always being present with us. We praise you for your work in the early church, giving us an example of how to form and shape disciples. If our work becomes hard, God, call us back to you, so that we might refocus on who we are, and whose we are. By your Spirit, may you shape and mold us into faithful disciples of Jesus Christ. Amen.*

## Chapter at a Glance

### GOALS

- To identify all the ministry activities in your church.

- To determine if, and how, each one contributes to making disciples for Jesus Christ.

- To gather input on the above from a larger contingent of the congregation.

- To begin the thought process, for both the team and the congregation, on what areas need more focus in order to more fully fulfill the mission.

## TIMEFRAME SUGGESTIONS

You may choose to have a separate session and invite participants from the congregation for the ministry listing activity.

## POSSIBLE FORMAT

- Read the centering prayer together, or have the facilitator read while the team meditates

- Work through *Bible Study: Practices of Growth* together

- Ask team members to make a list of every activity in the church they can think of (have two or three people capturing on newsprint).

- Review the mission of the congregation and the definition of a disciple that the team developed at a recent session. Post these where they can be seen.

- Using the identifying letters given in the chapter, or some other ones you create, evaluate your list:

  ■ Determine who is served by each "thing" on the list

  ■ Determine if each "thing" is contributing to making disciples of Jesus Christ

    — If yes, list how it is contributing (they most likely won't be able to answer all of these)

  ■ Identify any patterns emerging amongst the activities you evaluate

- If possible, leave this "wall" of activities where team members can review it between now and the next session, or capture the list in a handout that team members can have in the next day or two

  ■ Have team members continue to think about how each activity of the church does or does not fulfill the mission

  ■ Have them think about the areas your church needs to focus on in order to make disciples of Jesus Christ

- Close in prayer, in whatever way is appropriate

## Individual Preparation

What is the mission of the local church again?

***The mission of the Church is to make disciples of Jesus Christ.***

(And lest you forget, you'll be reading those words again and again throughout this book!)

In chapter 2, you struggled with a functional definition of a disciple—just what a disciple of Jesus Christ is and what a disciple of Jesus Christ does. Keep in mind that your definition of a disciple is "open"—that means you can change, adapt, adjust, and refine that definition as you continue developing your disciple-formation process. Just as persons are always changing, so is a functional definition of a disciple of Jesus Christ always changing. But those changes are changes in emphasis; they are not changes in fundamental and basic concepts.

Want a metaphor of sorts? Maybe a working definition of a disciple of Jesus Christ is something like a kaleidoscope. You look through a kaleidoscope and twist it to see wonderful designs and shapes. Remember that although you see different designs and shapes through the kaleidoscope, it is the same bits of colored glass that make all those shapes and designs. So it is with a definition of a disciple of Jesus Christ. The fundamental characteristics of what a disciple is and what a disciple does are unchanging, but the arrangements and concentration of those characteristics may change according to the situation of the moment.

So that brings us to the subject matter of this chapter.

How are you doing?

That is, how is your church, your congregation, doing in terms of making disciples of Jesus Christ?

If you say that your congregation is doing all it possibly can, that your congregation is very effective in making disciples of Jesus Christ, and that your congregation can do nothing more to make disciples of Jesus Christ, then you don't need this workbook. (And may the Judge of all have pity on you and your congregation.)

But if you feel that some opportunities for disciple making are still open to your congregation, that your congregation is really not doing all it can to make disciples of Jesus Christ, then read on.

*Note: The following should be done with the team. As an additional option, you may choose to repeat this activity with a larger group.* Now here's where you need some other members of your congregation. Remember when we said that this book is not intended for one person to read and put into practice? Here's a perfect example of that.

Gather members of your congregation, including members of your team. Get a crowd! (Yes, a crowd in a large membership congregation will be more than a crowd in a congregation with few members. But figure that six persons is an absolute minimum for this to work.) Welcome everyone, have some refreshments, make some small talk, open with prayer, and thank everyone for coming.

When everyone is ready to begin, jot down on a chalkboard, white board, or newsprint—or on good-sized "sticky notes"—all the "things" your congregation does—the activities, the programs, the ministries of your congregation. Get everyone involved in this process. Just ask all the folks present to call out the individual programs, activities, ministries, and anything and everything else you do as a church and congregation. Don't leave anything out. List everything. You might even want two or three persons jotting down on the board, newsprint, or sticky notes what folks are calling out so that nothing is lost. Once this gets "rolling," everyone will start talking at once.

Want some starters? You conduct services of worship. You have a Sunday School. You may have organizations for women, men, youth. You hold a rummage sale each year. You take up a special collection in December for the needy. Your annual fish fry is famous throughout the community. You send kids to church camp in the summer. You conduct a Vacation Bible School with a couple of other congregations. You have a volunteer choir that seeks to make a "joyful noise unto the Lord."

Keep going. Keep going. What else are you doing? Don't stop now. List every idea that is put forward. If you're not sure something belongs on the list, the answer is that it does; put it down.

A few folks involved in this process are going to start remembering some of the things you used to do as a congregation. "We used to have a car wash and bake sale, but we don't do that anymore." "Remember when a couple of our members went on that mission trip a few years ago?" "We tried Sunday night services quite some time ago, but they didn't go over too well, so we dropped them when the new pastor came."

Put them down. List them all. Get them up there on the board or newsprint.

A hint: Don't cut this sharing time short. Make sure everyone has plenty of time to think about all the things your congregation does. If someone hasn't spoken up too much, call on that person gently. "Don, what are you thinking? You look like you have something on your mind." "Mrs. Johnson, you've been in this church a long time. What are some of the things the church did when you were a youngster here?"

Don't, *do not*, ever evaluate anyone's comments or contributions! Just put them down. Nothing will kill this process more quickly that someone saying, "I don't think that belongs on this list." (Notice we haven't suggested a heading or title for this list; that's because titles and headings sometimes restrict free-wheeling brainstorming.)

You'll be able to tell when the contributions to the list begin to slow down a bit. Thank everyone for the ideas and thoughts, invite them to fill their coffee cups and grab some cookies, but remind them as they do that they can add to this list any time. If someone thinks of something that needs to go on the list, fine. Get it up there. Interrupt and get it on the board.

Now comes the harder part.

You as a whole group are going to evaluate each item on this list. You're not going to evaluate persons or what persons have said; you're not going to evaluate people's memories or understandings. You're going to evaluate that long list of "things" that your congregation does.

And here's a suggestion for how you're going to do that.

First, remind everyone of the mission of the Church. What was it again? Right. *To make disciples of Jesus Christ.* Then remind everyone of the definition of disciple that you developed at your last time together. In fact, it might be a good idea to post that definition somewhere where all can see it.

You don't have a fancy single sentence definition of disciple? Great! Post where all can see it your working, in-process, definition of a disciple, even if is only a beginning list of characteristics of a disciple

Now the objective of your next activity is to determine if each "thing" your congregation is doing is indeed making disciples of Jesus Christ. But a simple yes or no will not suffice. Develop your own set of symbols or evaluative descriptors. Here's one of many possible ways you could do this.

Alongside each item on your list (and hopefully it's a long list!) put one of these sets of letters or symbols:

**AMD** This thing that we as a church do *actively makes disciples* of Jesus Christ. That's what this activity is designed and intended to do. That's all it is intended to do. We as a congregation do this "thing" simply to make disciples of Jesus Christ. Example: A weekly Bible study in a prison.

**MDS** *Makes disciples secondarily*. What's that mean? It means that this activity is not designed for you as a congregation to make disciples directly but by your doing this "thing," some persons may become disciples. Example: Contributing money as a congregation to the local agency that helps the homeless.

**FOB** stands for *for our benefit*. These are the things the church does for the benefit of its own members, often for fun and fellowship. The regular fifth Sunday covered dish dinner might be an example of this. And, no, there's nothing at all wrong with a congregation doing things FOB.

**TPB** You know what that indicates. Those letters stand for *to pay bills*. These are the things a congregation does to pay its bills, to make building improvements or additions to the building fund, or, perhaps, to share some income with missionaries or helping agencies. The annual church fair, the rummage sale, and the car wash might be examples of this. Here's a hint: *TPB*'s are those activities in and through which you as a congregation ask other people outside the congregation to help support the church.

You say you can't remember all these letters? OK. Use some numbers or symbols or whatever works for you. How about a dollar sign ($) for those things you do to raise money for the church, the word *us* for those things you do just for the benefit of the members of the congregation, and perhaps a cross (✝) for those things that are specifically aimed at making disciples.

You've thought of some other ways to describe activities and things you do? Great! Add them and use them. Use as many as half a dozen or so categories, just so everyone understands each category. Sure, put up new or different categories as you go along, and move some of the "things" around from category to category as new categories are suggested.

Here's a warning: Some things are not going to fall neatly into one or another category.

What about Sunday morning worship, for example? You do that for the benefit of the church members and you hope that church members will grow in discipleship as a result of participating in worship. But whether or not your services of worship are primarily for your own benefit or are genuinely aimed at making disciples depends on how open, *how honestly open*, your services of worship are to the newcomer; the stranger; the person who looks, acts, and is different from the rest of you; how open your services are to those who speak a different language or come from another culture or country. Struggle with this; it's not easy.

So what do you do with these "things" that don't fit neatly into just one category? Don't worry. Put them in every category in which they seem to fit. But don't stretch too far! Yes, a person might start coming to your church because of your lawn fair in the Spring, but the purpose of your lawn fair is probably not to make disciples; it is to raise money for the church, right?

Lump all the items that fit into one category together until you have several clusters of items clustered together on the wall or board.

Here's another twist to try on your list of "things" that your church does. After you have generally lumped all those "things" into categories of some sort, go back and mark each "thing" with some sort of symbol of your choosing to designate what some would call "the target audience" for this thing. In other words, is this something you as a church do for children? For youth? For young adults? For middle adults? For older adults? For families? For single adults? For everyone? Of course, much of what you do is for everyone, but be honest here. For example, is the focus of your Sunday School children? Does your United Methodist Women include many young women? What does your church offer young, single, adult, college students?

What are you noticing here as a result of all these items arranged under categories? Which categories or clusters contain the most items? Which contain the least? Is your church undertaking more "things" to, say, raise money for the church or to actively make disciples? Is your church engaged in more activities primarily for the benefit of the members of your congregation or primarily to introduce others outside the congregation to Jesus Christ and his will for their lives? Of course, sheer numbers of items in one or another category do not necessarily suggest that that category receives the greatest attention from your congregation —but it's a pretty good indication of just where your priorities as a congregation might be.

Which age levels seem to be receiving the greatest attention from your congregation? Or to put this another, perhaps more important, way: Which age levels or living situations seem to receive little attention in your congregation? (Don't say, "This age level, because we don't have many persons of this age level in our congregation." The natural response to that statement then is, "Maybe you don't have many persons of that age level in your congregation because you're not offering persons of this age level anything to invite them and engage them." Yes, it's the old "chicken or egg" question, but think about it; it's important.)

By now, everyone's head is swimming, or should be. (If heads are not swimming, you haven't taken this seriously.) Time to break for this session, but leave the group with a couple of assignments.

First, can you leave the items on the wall or board until your next session? Invite the group to review the "wall" between now and the group's next session. Encourage them to add more "things" your church does, and to place these things in the categories in which they belong. Ask folks to study the categories carefully. What do the numbers and kinds of things in each category say about your congregation? What messages do the numbers and kinds of things in each category convey to those inside the church? And to those who may be outside the church looking in?

Second, based on this work on your congregation's "things," and the categories you've placed these things within, in what areas does your church need to focus and concentrate in order to make disciples of Jesus Christ? Ask folks to think along these terms:

"If we were going to be serious about making disciples of Jesus Christ we'd be doing more of this . . . and less of this . . . "

"If we want to be about the mission of the church, we need to pay much more attention to this . . . "

"One area where we need to concentrate in order to make disciples of Jesus Christ is . . . "

"We seem to be spending a lot of time and energy doing . . . when we should be spending more time and energy doing . . . to fulfill the mission of the church."

Get the idea? Don't lock persons into these sentence stems but use these sentence stems to get ideas flowing. Hang on to this work to come back to later. At your next session, you'll be doing some "visioning" based on what you've discovered about your congregation's ministries.

## The Role of the Team

The team's primary responsibility at this stage is to identify the current disciple-formation process, and measure it against the Church's mission.

## The Role of the Pastor

The pastor needs to be available to receive congregational input. In addition, the pastor should continue to cast the vision.

## The Role of the Congregation

The congregation's responsibility is to provide input about the current reality. The congregation needs to be open and honest about how ministries have helped them grow in their journey of discipleship. The congregation must be flexible and open to the possibility of bringing closure to ineffective ministry and to the possibility of new ministries.

## Check the Emotional Climate

Naming the current reality of a congregation's disciple formation process is a pivotal point of your work. As you assess the current reality, it may provide energy as you celebrate life-giving ministries and what works in the current context. You may need to harness this energy toward fine-tuning the present disciple-formation process. Sometimes, facing the current reality can be demoralizing to a congregation. A "reality check" can show a congregation that they do some, little, or no ministry toward the formation of disciples. You'll want to recognize for the congregation that forming and implementing a disciple-formation process will take time, and that they need not expect to move through the process in a year; it will take a lifetime.

As the team and/or larger group assesses the current reality, conflict may arise. Be aware that assessment often makes people protective of the ministries in which they are involved. As you evaluate the effectiveness of ministries, you may need to strategize how to provide closure to both ministries and the people carrying out the ministry.

# Going Deeper

## *Optional Exercise*

You may wish to expand the exercise on p. 52 by expanding the crowd to include other persons from within the life of your congregation that are not on the team addressing the following:

## *Assessing the Current Reality*

Thus far, you've articulated a definition of what a disciple is. With that definition, you formed the practices, or habits, of disciples. You have shown where the congregation spends time and resources. As the team looks at those ministries, some tough questions need to be asked:

- Are there people we aren't reaching?

- Does our current process allow for multiple entry points?

- Do our ministries move people further along in practicing their faith?

- What ministries do we engage in that take both time and resources, but do not contribute to the formation of disciples? Should we discontinue those ministries?

- How does our current process support God's vision for us? Are there ways we could improve?

- Do we own resources that contribute to disciple formation, but aren't currently being used?

Remember, not everything a congregation does in ministry contributes to the formation of disciples. As you answer these questions, and move forward in planning and implementing your disciple-formation process, be aware that you will receive resistance from members of the congregation. They have associations with some ministries that may be discontinued, and they will ask questions like "Why is *my* ministry being cut?" or "Why don't you appreciate me and the work I've done?" You'll want to deal with those questions from a missional perspective, reminding them that the mission of the church is to make disciples of Jesus Christ; you'll also want to do it in a compassionate way, showing them God's love in the midst of their anger, pain, and disappointment.

## Additional Resources

There are many ways to identify what your church currently does to form disciples. Mark Lau Branson's *Memories, Hopes, and Conversations* (The Alban Institute, 2004) may be helpful.

*Listening to God* (The Alban Institute, 2001) also has a helpful exercise (#4, p. 131-132) that helps people name where they've seen God in their midst, and in the midst of the congregation.

## Before Moving On

- If you decided to repeat the ministry listing exercise with a larger group, schedule and hold this session prior to moving on to chapter 5. Capture the responses with this group in a handout to be compared with the responses of the team.

(Handout)

## CHAPTER 4 BIBLE STUDY

# PRACTICES OF GROWTH

Engage the team in a Bible study on Acts 2:37-47. You might also use this Bible study with the group you gather together on p. 52. You might use the following questions to guide discussion on the passage.

1. In this passage, Peter has just finished his sermon, and people are moved to believe in Jesus Christ. The rest of the passage reflects their path of growth. Where do you see your journey with Jesus reflected in this passage?

2. Verses 41 and 42 describe the numbers who repented, were baptized, and became believers. Those verses also describe the practices of faith those disciples engaged in on a regular basis. Which of those practices are you engaged in, and in what practices do you lack regular engagement?

3. Verses 43-47 describe life among the believers. There are many more practices listed. Which practices do you find the most difficult? Which are easy for you?

4. The practices of the early church show us who we are to be as disciples, and who we are to be as the church. Engagement in those practices was, in a sense, the engagement in a disciple-formation process. How might you incorporate practices such as these in a disciple-formation process that works in your local context?

# WHERE DO WE WANT TO GO?

Here is where team members pause to focus, discern, and envision what God is calling your church to do. This discernment will happen in the context of reflection on Scripture, your mission, your vision, and your core values, and on the answers to a series of questions.

## Centering Prayer

*Wise and truthful God, you lay the path ahead for us, that we might know your will. Guide and direct us as we seek to discover the path. We want to see who you envision us to be. Help us to stop, listen, and hear your voice. Be the lamp for our feet and the light leading us to see you at the end of the path. We pray in Jesus' name, who is the Way, the Truth, and the Life. Amen.*

## Chapter at a Glance

### GOALS

- Determine where God is calling your church to go in working with this disciple-formation process.

- Develop a vision of what your church would look like if it were seriously focused on making disciples for Jesus Christ.

- Develop a vision statement

- Consider the use of a metaphor in developing your disciple-formation process.

## SUGGESTED TIMEFRAMES

This chapter will most likely take more than one session.

## POSSIBLE FORMAT

- Read the centering prayer together, or have the facilitator read while the team meditates

- Review with the team where this journey has taken us so far:

  ■ We're on a Mission!

  — Read again Matthew 28:16-20 and discuss what the mission of your church is, and what it means to make disciples for Jesus Christ

  ■ What's a Disciple?

  — Review the definition your team developed for a disciple; does this still fit? Do you still feel good about your definition?

  ■ Looking Around

  — Briefly discuss John Wesley's disciple-formation process, and one of the current church processes you reviewed, and dialogue about the things you learned from them

  ■ What Are We Doing?

  — Discuss what your team learned about your church as you listed the various ministries and activities you offer, and how those do or do not contribute to making disciples for Jesus Christ.

- Introduce the concepts of vision and vision statements

  ■ Vision is a mental picture of where you want to be at a certain time in the future; vision statement is a concise description of that place.

- Lead the *Lectio Divina* Bible Study found at the end of the chapter. The team may choose a passage to use for this. Some suggestions would be:

- Proverbs 29:18 (Where there is no vision . . .)

- Isaiah 43:19 (Behold, I do a new thing . . .)

- John 15:1-17 (I am the true vine . . .)

- A passage the team has worked with previously in this process

- Allow enough time for this study, even if it means that it takes the whole session. Just plan a second session for further visioning. When the team comes back together after each one has engaged in *lectio divina* (either this session or next), invite everyone to share what they discovered, as they invited the spirit of God to help them see the future. (Capture people's comments on newsprint.)

• Review briefly again what a vision statement is. Hand out copies of "Guidelines for a Healthy Disciple-Formation Process," found at the back of this chapter on p. 93.

• Review again the mission of your church.

• Ask the questions (and capture answers on newsprint):

- If our congregation were serious, really serious, about making disciples of Jesus Christ, what would our congregation be doing in five years?

- What would our congregation be doing that it IS doing now?

- What would our congregation be doing that it is NOT doing now and perhaps has never done?

- What are we doing now that we probably wouldn't be doing in five years because these things do not contribute to making disciples of Jesus Christ?

- Start your vision statement something like this: "In five years, our congregation will . . . ." Tips for the team:

— Instead of a simple sentence to complete that statement, use a series of sentence completions, perhaps numbered or bulleted in some way.

— List target audiences first, then list under each target audience a particular and specific ministry that you want to be doing in five years to reach that audience.

— Consider what kinds of ministries your congregation could and should undertake to reach out to them and to create for them the opportunities where they may become disciples of Jesus Christ.

— See additional questions to consider under the "Going Deeper" section.

■ Although it will be subject to revision in subsequent weeks, work to get a detailed vision statement written down.

• Invite the group to be thinking about a metaphor or image that might inform and communicate the disciple-formation process, if one has not already emerged.

• Close the session in prayer, in whatever way seems appropriate.

## Individual Preparation

That last session was kind of fun, wasn't it? If your congregation is like many congregations, you discovered that you do a lot; your calendar is filled with many "things." But you may have also discovered that some of the things you do—perhaps many of the things you do—are not very effective in fulfilling the mission of the church.

What was that mission of the Church again?

***The mission of the Church—your church—is to make disciples of Jesus Christ.***

We've also said that the Church carries out that mission by doing "things;" that is, by engaging in ministries.

(By the way, a congregation is not involved in "programs." Programs are what we watch on television and activities undertaken by social clubs and organizations. The church is involved in *ministries*. A working definition of *ministries* might be: *Those activities by and through which persons both within and outside the congregation grow in Christian faith and discipleship.* Does that definition of ministries cause a bit of an "ouch"? Every congregation comes to realize sooner or later that some of the things on which it spends its time, resources, and energy do not contribute to growth in Christian faith and discipleship. The classic question then is: "Why are we doing these things?" Better have some good answers! We'll be talking about the church's ministries throughout the rest of this workbook; we'll leave the word "programs" to other agencies.)

You've identified all the things your congregation does, or at least most of them, and you've grouped those according to categories you've set up. You've also identified what the marketers call the "target audience" for those "things," and you've probably come to realize that some kinds of persons are not included in your congregation's ministries. What kinds of persons? We talked of age levels and marital status, to name just two, but your group probably thought of more, such as socio-economic level, educational background, church (or lack of church) background, persons new to the faith, those ready to go deeper, and so on.

Now where do we go from here?

Well, to use some techniques that are widely used in a variety of enterprises, developing a *vision statement* might be a good place to start.

Hold on. Don't start writing yet!

Make sure the people on the team understand what a vision statement is, at least in the ways we're using that term here.

Put most simply, *a vision statement is a statement that describes where a group wants to be at a certain time in the future.* It's up to the group to decide what that certain future time is, and it is up to the group to define in some detail just where the team wants to be in that period of time.

Let's use a simple example: If your congregation were serious, really serious, about making disciples of Jesus Christ, what would your congregation be doing in five years?

- What would your congregation be doing that it is doing now?

- What would your congregation be doing that it is not doing now and perhaps has never done?

- What are you doing now that you probably wouldn't be doing in five years because these things do not contribute to making disciples of Jesus Christ?

Get the idea?

A vision statement is a detailed description of where we want to be and what we want to be doing in five or ten years (you set the time frame). But it is a description of where we want to be and what we want to be doing *as seen through a particular "lens."* And what is the "lens" through which we look at the future? Easy! Our old friend, the mission of the Church: Making disciples of Jesus Christ.

Some writers have said the mission is like the frame of the window through which we look at the future. You use the metaphor that communicates most effectively with you. In other words, a vision statement does not describe *everything* about what the future will be like in five years. Rather, a vision statement describes what we want the future to look like *in terms of our mission, in terms of making disciples of Jesus Christ.*

A couple of examples: You may hope that the church gets new choir robes in the next five years. Your vision is "new robes for the choir." But if you look at the future through the lens of the mission statement—making disciples of Jesus Christ—does the expenditure of energy and resources on choir robes "pay off" in terms of fulfilling the mission of the congregation as much as, say, an active bus ministry in the public housing project across town?

Your vision for five years might be a new fellowship hall where you can hold covered dish dinners for the congregation and have a place for your children and youth to play basketball. But if that new building is seen through the "lens" of the mission statement, you might modify that vision to include setting up a ministry of meals and overnight accommodations for the homeless in your community and holding "open gymnasium" three nights a week so that all the neighborhood children can have a place to play and "hang out" that is safe, supervised, and Christian, a place where the love of Christ can be put into action.

Are you beginning to get the idea here?

Does new carpeting in the ladies' parlor contribute to making disciples as much as volunteering at the local women's and children's shelter? Does the men's annual fishing trip contribute as much to making disciples as challenging those men to take some fatherless kids fishing on a regular basis, and demonstrating the love of Christ in the process?

When we dream about the future and start to paint a picture of what we want it to look like, we paint that picture in terms of the mission of the church, in terms of making disciples of Jesus Christ.

Does everyone on the team get the idea? Good. Then let's proceed.

First, set a time frame for your vision statement. You're looking through the lens of the mission statement, but you need to determine just how far out into the future you're looking. A couple of hints:

If you look at the immediate future—say six months or a year—you and your congregation may grow frustrated with your inability to bring about all that you'd like to accomplish in six months or a year. But if you look at the really long-range future—say ten to fifteen years—then everyone can sit back and say, "Don't worry; we have plenty of time to get started on those ministries." And often the hidden agenda is, "We'll wait until we get some new and active members to get started on those ministry ideas." You know what happens. The new active members do not come. Why? Because you as a congregation are not doing anything to make disciples of Jesus Christ. You're right; it is a vicious cycle.

So what's a good time frame? Most writers in this area suggest three to five years, with five years being most often cited. Five years is a manageable amount of time, but not so much time that you can afford to put things off until later. Five years is a reasonable amount of time to expect that the core members of your congregation will still be a part of your church. Five years is enough time for some significant things, really significant things, to take place in your congregation.

So you might start your vision statement something like this, "In five years, our congregation will . . ." Now complete that statement.

With a single sentence completion? Not necessarily. A single sentence completion does not really say anything. Avoid the temptation to say, "In five years, our congregation will be making disciples of Jesus Christ." Of course, you should be doing that in five years, but that simple a vision statement provides no clues, no ideas, and no directions as to how you're going to fulfill that vision. So instead of a simple sentence to complete that statement, use a series of sentence completions, perhaps numbered or "bulleted" in some way.

One way to get your group started on this is to go back to that list of "target audiences," folks you identified as not being served (or served very well) by your church. List them first, then list under each "target audience" a particular and specific ministry that you want to be doing in five years to reach that audience.

One possible example:

In five years, our congregation will

Minister directly to post high school young adults through:

- A Sunday School class designed especially for them.

- A bi-monthly *"Christian fun and fellowship"* night to which our post high school young adults can and will invite their friends.

- A weekly early morning breakfast Bible study built around the needs, interests, concerns, and opportunities of post high school young adults.

- A monthly mission project designed by and for post high school young adults, including (but not limited to) special ministries with young persons at the local homeless shelter.

Get the idea? Think about those persons in your congregation, and more important, those in your community, who are not being served (or are being under-served) by your congregation. What kinds of ministries could and should your congregation undertake to reach out to them and to create for them the opportunities where they may become disciples of Jesus Christ? Get the team involved in imaging ways to serve these various kinds of persons. Get ideas up; have your "recorders" ready to jot down ideas on the newsprint or chalkboards. You might spend a couple of moments in silence, asking folks to jot down their own individual ideas, before opening the session to brainstorming. This way, everyone should have at least one or two ideas to contribute. Don't be afraid of posing a question to get the ball rolling: If we were going to get really serious about reaching out to post high school young adults in our community with the Gospel of Jesus Christ, what are some of the things we would be doing?

Go through this process with the several kinds of audiences you as a group identified.

Dream! Imagine! Reach out! But don't, *don't* let anyone critique or comment on ideas as they are suggested. This is not the time for naysayers or critics. This is not the time for those whose favorite line is, "It'll never work here." This is not the time for those who want to argue, "It's not in the budget," or "How could we afford to do that?"

---

"The real antichrist is he who turns the wine of an original idea into the water of mediocrity." Eric Hoffer[1]

---

This is also a great time to be thinking about an image or metaphor that might arise in the discernment/visioning of the Team. A picture or symbol that represents God's future for your church will speak deeply to many people. In chapter 6, you will be invited to use this image or metaphor in the development of your disciple formation process.

The goal here is to dream, dream, and dream some more! If you are serious about making disciples of Jesus Christ over the next five years, what will you be doing? Don't worry if your list

1. Eric Hoffer, *Reflections on the Human Condition* (New York: Harper & Row, 1973).

gets long and even longer. You will have plenty of time to combine ideas, set priorities, and maybe prune the list a bit. A vision statement is not a single statement or a couple of sentences. It is your marching orders. It is an outline of who you will be and what you will be doing in five years. It is a detailed picture of just what your congregation will be like in five years. It is the goal toward which you are striving. It is that mountain peak you see in the distance and upon the top of which you are determined to stand, by God's grace and help!

## Role of the Team

Your role is to lead the visioning process through discernment. Team members should listen actively to one another, ask hard questions of the team, and be willing to push the edges of conventional "church thinking". Throughout this step, the team should always be prayerfully discerning if this is truly a vision from God.

## Role of the Pastor

The pastor may need to take the lead on teaching and equipping the team for discernment and visioning. Push the team, when it's appropriate, to dig deeper in seeking God's vision, and give the team permission to push the boundaries. Help the team keep their focus on God. The pastor also should be actively involved in articulating the mission of the church throughout the discernment of the vision.

## Role of the Congregation

The congregation's role is to participate in the visioning process as invited by the team, and to participate in places and ways to test the vision as provided by the team. The congregation needs to be encouraged in a spirit of patience and honest engagement.

## Check the Emotional Climate

The person on the team who is charged with this will need to keep a watchful spirit for those who may begin feeling frustrated by the amount of time it could take to envision your future. Don't allow the team to rush, and continue to assure team members and the congregation that this simply will take time to discern and seek consensus. Stay calm, and be a non-anxious presence.

## Going Deeper

Here are some additional questions and invitations to help you grow in clarity about what your disciple-formation process will mean to your church, as you engage in discernment:

- What are the needs in our community? What does our church need to be for such a time as this?

- What could be ahead for our church as we take seriously the call to make and grow disciples?

- What would our church look like if people were really living as disciples, as we've defined disciple?

- What is God calling our church to do?

- What does God want our Christian community look like in five, ten, or twenty years?

- What, in our church's history, speaks to our future?

- How would our community be different if our church folks were living out our definition of disciple in their daily lives?

This part of the discernment process may take several weeks to complete. Give yourselves permission to teach and equip the team for discernment & Christian conversation, so this step can happen appropriately. And give yourselves permission to take the time you need to accomplish this step.

Discernment is not about taking a vote, thereby creating winners and losers. It's about honest speaking and honest listening. It's about hearing God's voice through others. It's about agreeing with God's direction and then moving forward together. This is a very sacred time for your team. Don't misuse it; stay attentive to the spirit of God as it comes through the members of your team in their reflection.

## Additional Resources

To read more about the ancient practice of meditative Scripture reading, refer to *A Faithful Future, vol. 2;* section 6, pages 67 – 78. This passage, written by Susan W. N. Ruach, provides excellent explanation of the practice, and will dive deeper into the movements of *lectio divina.*

For help with group discernment consider:

*Practicing Our Faith,* ed. by Dorothy C. Bass, Jossey-Bass (1997); chapter 8, "Discernment" by Frank Rogers Jr.

*Discerning God's Will Together,* by Danny E. Morris and Charles M. Olsen, Upper Room Books (1997); chapter 4.

*Transforming Church Boards,* by Charles M. Olsen, An Alban Institute Publication (1995); chapter 5.

## Before Moving On

- Capture any relevant newsprint items and put them in handout form for the next meeting.

- Consider whether there are any potential "land mines" in the conversation about what the church might or might not be doing five years from now, and determine if there are any proactive conversations that need to take place prior to the next session.

- If you decided not to do the exercise in chapter 4 with a larger group, and you now feel that might be necessary, schedule and hold that meeting prior to moving on to chapter 6 content.

## CHAPTER 5 BIBLE STUDY

# *LECTIO DIVINA*

*Lectio divina* means sacred reading or holy reading. Engaging in *lectio divina* is like inviting God to show us or tell us whatever we need to be shown or to hear. First practiced by the Desert Mothers and Fathers in the fourth century, *lectio divina* includes four movements: reading, meditation, prayer, and contemplation.

The passage you choose to use for this Bible study is up to the Team. You may want to use a passage you've worked with previously in this process, or maybe even to give each team member a different passage from among those that have been suggested during the process. Be open to the leading of the Spirit in making this decision.

Set aside thirty to sixty minutes to practice the *lectio divina*. Make yourself comfortable in a place where you will not be disturbed. Take some deep, cleansing breaths, and invite God to grant wisdom and insight to you and your team as you engage in the *lectio divina*.

**Movement 1: Reading.** After identifying the Scripture passage you'll be using, read the passage aloud in a quiet voice. Read it slowly. You might have the passage available in different translations, and invite people to take turns reading it so you can hear various interpretations. Let the words you hear quench your spirit. As the reader(s) read, listen for God. Listen for a word or phase that "grabs" you.

**Movement 2: Meditation.** Meditation is thinking deeply about something, in this case the Scripture passage. What was it about that particular spot in the passage that "grabbed" you? Try to put yourself into the story as one of the characters, or as the speaker. What are you experiencing as you immerse yourself in the passage? What is this passage about? How do you personally relate to what you're reading? What is God trying to say to you or invite you to in this passage? It might be useful to write down some of your ideas as you meditate.

**Movement 3: Prayer.** Engage in prayer in whatever is your typical style. Share with God your thoughts, feelings, what you've discovered in the times of reading and meditation, whatever comes to mind and heart. Remember to listen too. You may wish to write your prayers. Spend whatever amount of time seems appropriate for you. Then move on to the last movement.

**Movement 4: Contemplation.** This movement is about being still in God, giving our thinking process over to God, while our spirits worship God. Begin with two or three deep, cleansing breaths. Then start to repeat a word prayer. This might be a phrase from Scripture, or maybe the words that "grabbed" you in the first movement. It might be a one sentence prayer or a favorite name for God. Use this "word prayer" to redirect your contemplation whenever other thoughts come into your mind. End this time with care. Slowly come back to your conscious state, perhaps pray The Lord's Prayer, whatever seems appropriate for you.

# HOW WILL WE GET THERE?

At this point, you know what your church currently does to facilitate disciple formation, and you are trying to move from your current reality toward God's vision for your Church. As you work through this chapter, the team will develop a plan to improve your disciple-formation process.

## Centering Prayer

*God of the past, present, and future, we are grateful for your presence in our midst. Our work sometimes seems difficult and tedious, but you have been right with us in the midst of it all. We thank you for your abiding love that keeps us focused on you and your vision for us. Help us to keep our work faithful to you. May it embrace your mission and vision, and may it bring about the making of lifelong disciples of Jesus Christ, in whose name we pray. Amen.*

## Chapter at a Glance

### GOALS

- Evaluate your tentative plans (vision statement, ministry activities, etc.) against the characteristics of successful disciple-formation systems to determine effectiveness.

- Develop a comprehensive plan to create or improve the disciple-formation process for your church.

- Decide what metaphor, if any, you want to use to describe and communicate the disciple-formation process.

## TIMEFRAME SUGGESTIONS

At first glance, it would seem that this is somewhat of a short chapter. However, this chapter could take multiple sessions. You may need one entire session on reviewing the stages of disciple formation, as this is an area where often individuals have widely varying opinions. You will most likely need a session identifying what is/should be offered in your church for each of the stages, once you've identified them. It may also take time to decide what you want to call the various stages in your disciple-formation process. Take your time with this section; it's critical that this is solid.

## POSSIBLE FORMAT

- Read the centering prayer together, or have the facilitator read while the group meditates

- Share together the Bible Study of Nicodemus on John 3:1-21.

- Review the handout "Identifying the Stages" at the end of this chapter. Work through this together, identifying the ministries you already have, or that you may have already decided to add at this point, determining where each of them fit in the stages and levels of discipleship. Celebrate what you're already doing! Now determine where there are gaps. What new ministries and opportunities do you want to add, or at least pursue adding? (Capture all this on newsprint.)

- Then have the group respond to each of these questions regarding your new vision (and capture on newsprint):

  - Is everyone clear about the church's mission?

  - Is our congregation growing in Christian faith and discipleship as we seek to make disciples?

  - Is our congregation participating in the wider community of faith, the connectional system, and in ecumenical efforts to make disciples of Jesus Christ?

- Is our congregation genuinely preaching shared leadership by recognizing that each person is a leader in her or his own right, that each has been given gifts for disciple formation by God?

- Is our disciple-formation process, including our vision statement, in line with these characteristics?

- How does our plan fit with our definition of a disciple?

- How does this process affect and effect transformation in the community and the world?

• Alert the team that the next step is to get the whole congregation on board. This, too, may take several sessions, as totally encompassing the congregation will not happen overnight. You may need several weeks just for this phase. Allow the time. Remember that you want a process that will accomplish the mission and make the vision into reality. The Going Deeper section is full of possibilities for continued evaluation.

• Close in prayer, in whatever way seems appropriate.

## Individual Preparation

*Whoa!*

You and the group are doing just fine! The ideas are flowing, the ministries are being described, enthusiasm is swelling. Wonderful! That's just what is supposed to happen.

But before the members of your congregation get deeply involved in the ministries they have described as parts of their vision statement, stop! Catch your breath. Pause again for prayer. And do a little evaluating.

Yes, United Methodists are famous for evaluating. We evaluate everything, including the evaluations of our evaluations! We can laugh about it among ourselves. But among the many things that John Wesley (one of those credited with the founding of what we know as The United Methodist Church) taught us was to be sure we are headed in the right direction before we go galloping down the road. Enthusiasm is wonderful; we need it; praise God for it. But enthusiasm needs at times to be tempered with careful review and evaluation; we need to be sure we are moving in the directions God really wants us to go, we need to be confident that the visions we have set for ourselves will truly take us where God is leading us.

And where do we want to go? (Trick question!) The answer again is: We want to make disciples of Jesus Christ! That is our mission. That's why we are here as a congregation. That is our reason for being. Because we are the church, we make disciples of Jesus Christ. It's what we do, and it is what we as a congregation have determined to do better and better as we as individuals and as a community continue to grow in Christian faith and discipleship ourselves.

So you have a tentative plan for making disciples. Many members of your congregation have had a hand in forming it. It's couched in the form of a vision statement—or more properly —a series of statements. And you are ready to dig in and make it happen so that five years from now you can celebrate your accomplishments and work on another plan.

Let's evaluate that overall plan a bit first to make sure it is consistent with what we know and mean by disciple making. And perhaps the best way to do this is to compare your plan with some of the major characteristics of the plans that have worked well in other churches and congregations.

A quick caveat, however: Your church and congregation cannot adopt another church's plan for ministries or for making disciples. The reasons are simple and obvious: Yours is a unique congregation in a unique community. No other church in all the world is exactly like your church, and no other community is exactly like your community. And should you be tempted to adopt another church's overall plan, remember, too, that that other church is absolutely unique. No other church in the world, including yours, is quite like that church whose plan you want to adopt and no other community is quite like the community in which that church is located.

So to put matters very bluntly: What worked for that other church will not work for your congregation! And what works for your congregation will not work for that other church! Sure, we can share ideas and insights, and we can profit from learning what others have done, we can develop and fine-tune our plan based on what we've learned from others. But your plan must be the plan for your church and your church alone! (By the way, that's the big reason why "canned" or "pre-packaged" church growth programs or courses seldom work. Sure, they worked in the congregations in which they were created, but those courses and programs seldom transfer perfectly to another setting. And yes, we're using that word "programs" here because that is what some of these mass-marketed, "perfect cure for what ails every congregation," schemes are. By all means, look at some of them, select what you can use in your setting, modify, and adapt. But focus on *your* congregation and *your* community; not on what worked somewhere else.)

What you *can* learn from other churches and congregations that have become successful in disciple making are some basic principles or characteristics, some "you have to give attention to these concerns to be successful" points, and some fundamental markers that will make your plan for disciple making work if followed and that will hinder your efforts if ignored.

Scholars and practitioners have studied successful disciple-making congregations from many angles, and the consensus seems to suggest that the following are some characteristics that lead to success in making disciples. Your task as a congregation, then, is to evaluate your plan against these characteristics to help make sure you are on the right track.

**1. Congregations that are successfully making disciples are congregations in which every member and constituent of the congregation knows and understands the mission of the church.** Everyone has a grasp on the nature of God's mission in the world, and because every member understands that, every member has a firm grip on what the congregations is called to be and do.

Did you notice some key elements here? In congregations that are successful in disciple making, everyone knows and understands what the church is about. An understanding of the mission of the church is not something just for the pastor or the lay leader or a few members of the governing board. It is not just a handful of Sunday School teachers and committee chairpersons who know the mission of the church. Everyone—children, youth, and adults—everyone knows what the church is about and what its mission is. No confusion, no uncertainty, no hedging. Ask any member of a congregation that is making disciples successfully what his or her church is about, and that member will immediately tell you that the church's mission is to make disciples of Jesus Christ. And most of them will tell you exactly what they as individuals are doing to make disciples because they know that's their job!

**2. Congregations that are successfully about disciple making are actively growing in discipleship themselves.** Who is growing in discipleship? Each member of the congregation *and* the congregation as a community! Becoming a disciple is not a "once and for all" matter. Becoming a disciple is a lifelong process both for individuals and for congregations. And congregations that are successful about disciple making pay attention to this lifelong process.

United Methodists believe in "sanctifying grace." That's the grace of God that enables each of us to grow in discipleship day by day and that's the grace of God that enables the community of faith, the congregation, to grow in discipleship day by day. This comes again from John Wesley, that English clergyman whose ideas have influenced the Methodist movement so much. Wesley taught that we grow in discipleship as a community and as individuals when we intentionally attend to acts of devotion, acts of justice, acts of worship, and acts of compassion. Congregations that are successful in making disciples attend to these means of grace. If we ignore sanctifying grace, ignore growth in discipleship on the part of the community of faith or the members of the congregation, then we will probably experience what has come to be called "burn-out." Folks and congregations must be nurtured themselves as they seek to nurture others.

**3. Congregations and individuals who are about making disciples of Jesus Christ are active participants in the community of faith.** That's easy for individuals. Persons are active members of a congregation. They attend Sunday School and worship, they partake of the sacraments, they are involved in Bible study and prayer groups, they may participate in ministries such as *Walk to Emmaus* or *Covenant Discipleship*, and they may be involved in many other ministries of the congregation.

But how is the whole congregation a participant in the community of faith? The community of faith for a congregation is the church universal and the church triumphant. The congregation's community of faith is the broader and wider community of faithful Christians in the greater community, be they United Methodists or members of other denominations.

Another of John Wesley's teachings is that we as United Methodists are part of a connectional church; that is, each congregation is intimately related to every other congregation, for we can do so much more together than we could possibly dream of doing alone. The United Methodist Church has no place for "Lone Rangers," be they individuals or congregations. We are connected; we work together with our Christian brothers and sisters everywhere. The congregation does not stand alone; it is supported by the entire connectional system of the church and in turn supports the entire connectional system of the church. A "stand-alone" congregation is isolated, self-centered, anxious, and intent on self-preservation. Such a congregation cannot be about making disciples.

**4. Congregations that are successfully making disciples are leader-centered congregations.** But the amazing thing about such congregations is that they have as many leaders as they have members! Every member of such a congregation takes a leading role of some form or another in the disciple-making process. The pastor does not do it all; the designated leadership teams do not do it all; the "old timers" do not do it all and the "newcomers" do not do it all. Everyone is seen as a leader with special gifts and skills, given to her or him by God, to be used in the disciple-making process. In short, God would not have called congregations and individuals to make disciples if God had not equipped congregations and individuals to do so.

So in disciple-making congregations, everyone has a part to play; everyone is crucial to the process. Everyone is a leader, for everyone—each one of whatever age—is called by God to take an important role in making disciples of Jesus Christ. That's why the emphasis in this workbook has been on involving the whole congregation and on giving every single idea or suggestion high value. Every member of the congregation has a vitally important part to play in making disciples; thus every one is a crucial leader!

---

Warning: Nothing can stifle disciple making more quickly than one person or a small group of persons claiming all responsibility and authority for the congregation's disciple-making efforts. Real leadership is always shared leadership!

---

**5. Congregations in which disciple making is working are congregations that have a plan designed by the members of the congregation for that specific congregation and that particular community.** No one says, "Let's go make disciples!" and leaves it at that. Successful congregations are intentional about how they are going to go about making disciples, just as you and your congregation are being intentional right now about a plan to make disciples.

So how does your vision statement and all the ideas connected with it look now?

- Is everyone clear about the church's mission?

- Is your congregation growing in Christian faith and discipleship as you seek to make disciples?

- Is your congregation participating in the wider community of faith, the connectional system, and in ecumenical efforts to make disciples of Jesus Christ?

- Is your congregation genuinely practicing shared leadership by recognizing that each person is a leader in her or his own right, for each has been given gifts for disciple formation by God?

- Is your vision statement in line with these characteristics?

---

One more brief word: Please go back to chapter 2 of this workbook and re-read and think about your definition of a disciple. That definition is the focus of your disciple-making activities. You are trying to help persons become what that definition describes by providing them with the experiences and the opportunities in which they can respond to Christ's call to discipleship.

This is not about numbers. Making disciples does not just mean getting more folks to come to your church. Anyone can increase attendance at a church by a wide variety of gimmicks and tricks. But just getting people to come to church is not making disciples. It is not fulfilling the definition of a disciple that you labored over in chapter 2.

Yes, getting people in church is important. Yes, church may be the place where persons encounter the living Christ and become disciples. Yes, attendance and membership are important. But they are not the "all in all."

Disciple making is.

Dr. Randall Alshire, executive director of the Council of Theological Schools, said in a videotape interview that membership growth is theologically neutral. By this he meant that sheer numbers alone are not the indicator of successful ministries of disciple making. Even very small congregations with little hope of increased attendance and membership can be (and are!) vitally involved in making disciples of Jesus Christ. Size is not the criterion; the definition of a disciple that you formulated is.

## Building for a New Reality

After you've spent time in discernment, and believe you have heard God's leading, begin working from your current reality. You may have already begun a pruning process, cutting back excess ministries that don't move people to grow deeper in spiritual practices. The team may need to engage in more pruning now.

As you move through this recommended pruning process, you must remember your congregation's context. You may need to prune ministries so that the pastor, leaders, and congregation aren't spread too thin. Remember some of those activities from Chapter 4 that aren't actively making disciples? Many times, quantity replaces quality in our culture, but when you're forming disciples, having quality ministries is more important than the number of ministries offered.

Remember that people will enter your church's disciple-formation process at various points.

Some may have just been introduced to Christ, and are hungry to learn more, but DISCIPLE I might not be a good entry point for them. Others may transfer to your congregation from another United Methodist church or another denomination and have already been engaged in a disciple formation process. How will those persons enter your congregation's disciple-formation process?

When you've discovered both resources and format, add these new ministries to the current process. You'll begin to see the process flowing together. Here are some next steps to take once the process takes shape:

- Determine how or if the image/metaphor fits into the improved disciple-formation process. What does it look like? How will it be used?

- Identify key components/opportunities for growth that can generate excitement, enthusiasm, and a sense of forward direction.

- Determine a timeline/strategy for implementation of the disciple-formation process.

- Determine what needs to happen to implement the disciple-formation process (gathering new resources; finding leaders for studies, small groups and ministry teams; times for ministries to occur; funding, etc.) *Note: chapter 7 will discuss promotion and launching of the process.*

- Determine if there are barriers to the disciple-formation process, and provide strategies to move beyond them. This may include dealing with resistance to pruning and change.

- Discern a form of self-assessment that helps people determine where they are in the disciple-formation process, as well as a point of entry.

- Determine if people need to know their specific stage of faith (see p. 44-45). Does it provide clarity, provide confusion, or create anxiety? Self assessments can be designed to identify stages for individuals, but they can also move people into the process by naming the current reality of their spiritual practices for themselves (i.e. people might identify how they are doing in the practice of prayer by responding to statements such as "I don't know how to pray."; or "I speak and listen to God on a daily basis.").

- As people identify where they can grow deeper, they will be able to step into the process that's appropriate for their current reality/stage of faith.

## The Role of the Team

A main priority is listening and discernment. Listen to and beyond the congregation. Spend considerable time in prayer, both before and during the development of the new disciple-formation process. During your work, communicate progress to the congregation on a regular basis, and listen for feedback. The more listening you do, the better the possibilities for people to own the process for themselves.

## The Role of the Pastor

The pastor has an important role as the disciple-formation process takes shape. The pastor needs to participate in the team's process, providing direction and support where needed. There may be times when the team's emotions are high, especially in dealing with resistance, and the pastor will need to minister to the team. The pastor must be open to change, and s/he must be willing to step forward and lead change. S/he serves as a primary mouthpiece to the congregation, and must be willing to communicate through letters, newsletter articles, sermons, and teaching. The pastor should also expect to deal with resistance to change, and can seek additional help.

## The Role of the Congregation

Throughout this process, the congregation may have needed to make adjustments in the way they think or act; the mission, definition of a disciple, and vision can cause this. In some respects, they have already experienced change. They will either be resistant to further change, indifferent, or they will expect change and look forward to it. On the whole, though, the congregation needs to be open to learning about the new disciple-formation process, and have a willingness to change.

## Check the Emotional Climate

You can expect the congregation's emotions to be high during this time in the development of your disciple-formation process. People will resist the changes taking place, if it hasn't already begun by this time, and they will ask questions based on emotions. Remember to redirect them toward the mission, but deal with them in a loving and caring way. People will also fear change. They live in a culture that constantly changes, and they look to the church as a bedrock, a place of stability. They need to be redirected to focus on Jesus Christ as their bedrock.

The team may experience some emotional anxiety at this point. You're in the midst of a difficult process, and as you hear feedback, try to maintain a non-anxious presence. If you are anxious, it will not help the congregation's anxiety level. Be ministers to each other, and support one another.

## Going Deeper

The notes and resources below can help as you evaluate your vision so far and begin to shift from current reality.

### *About Metaphors*

As the Team began working on a church-owned definition of a disciple, and as it discerned God's preferred future, an image may have started to form. If that is the case, you may want to now revisit your work from Chapter 5 for clarification. If it didn't happen at that time, now is the time to discover a metaphor or image for the process.

Here are some examples of how a metaphor might be used:

> At *Christ UMC and Riverside UMC* (East Moline and Moline, IL), the river serves as a potent image. The stages are supplemented by river language (testing the water, using a life preserver, swimming, diving deeper, riding the rapids, etc.) to help persons engage with what it means to be part of discipleship journey. Both churches have found their vision (though articulated in different ways) through the image of the river (since both churches serve communities found on the Mississippi River). See www.powerus.org

> *Brentwood UMC* in Nashville (TN) invites people to navigate the river with Christ. Their publications use river imagery, and their stages (Checking Out the Scene, Stepping in the Water, Diving Deeper, Riding the Rapids, and Going Fishing) invite persons to engage further in the river of life.

*Evangelical UMC* in Greenville, OH uses the image of the ocean as a means of discipleship for their congregation. Their stages are *Life on the Beach*, *Life on the Shoreline*, *Life in the Waves*, *Life When Your Feet Come Off the Bottom*, *Life Beyond the Breakers*, and *Life in the Deep*. They use imagery to show each stage/mark, showing a physical representation of a person at each stage.

These metaphors provide visual, mental, and emotional stimuli, or guides for the discipleship journey. Keep in mind that as you develop an image/metaphor, you will need to remember your context. The image/metaphor must be something to which the congregation can relate and own.

## Before Moving On

- Be sure you have taken the time necessary to fully develop the disciple-formation system, that the team can articulate it well, it can be clearly defined through a metaphor or other communication tool, that you have immersed your congregation in the sharing of this system, allowing your congregation time and opportunity to understand, articulate, and connect with the mission and purpose of this whole disciple-formation "movement" in the life of your church.

(Handout)

# MOVING TO A NEW REALITY: IDENTIFYING THE STAGES

So you've articulated a definition of what a disciple is. With that definition, you formed the practices, or habits, of disciples. You also have discerned what God's vision is for your church and for the particular mission of disciple formation in your context. You have also identified various markers or stages along the journey of discipleship.

Now is the time to assimilate all of these definitions and markers as you develop a tool to guide the direction of the disciple-formation process! There are many ways to do this, and the following suggestions are not exhaustive:

Suggestion 1: Using the information you've gathered, create a grid using the practices of a disciple, the United Methodist Church's core process, and/or the stages of faith. For example, a grid might look like this:

|  | Cautious | Curious | Committed | Professing | Inviting |
|---|---|---|---|---|---|
| Inviting |  |  |  |  |  |
| Welcoming |  |  |  |  |  |
| Nurturing |  |  |  |  |  |
| Sending |  |  |  |  |  |

In this example, stages of faith are placed across the top of columns, and the United Methodist Church's core process is placed at the beginning of each row. Remember, develop your own categories!

Another grid may look like this:

| | One-Hour Christians | Seeker Christians | Growing Christians | Maturing Christians | Core Ministry Christians |
|---|---|---|---|---|---|
| Practice #1 | | | | | |
| Practice #2 | | | | | |
| Practice #3 | | | | | |
| Practice #4 | | | | | |
| Practice #5 | | | | | |
| Practice #6 | | | | | |

In this example, stages of faith are placed across the top of columns, and the practices of a disciple, identified by your congregation, begin each row.

Suggestion #2: Use the information you've gathered to create a web or circle. Divide the web/circle into quadrants based on the discipleship practices the Team has discerned. You might then "layer" the circle to engage the stages or marks using different colors:

Bible Study

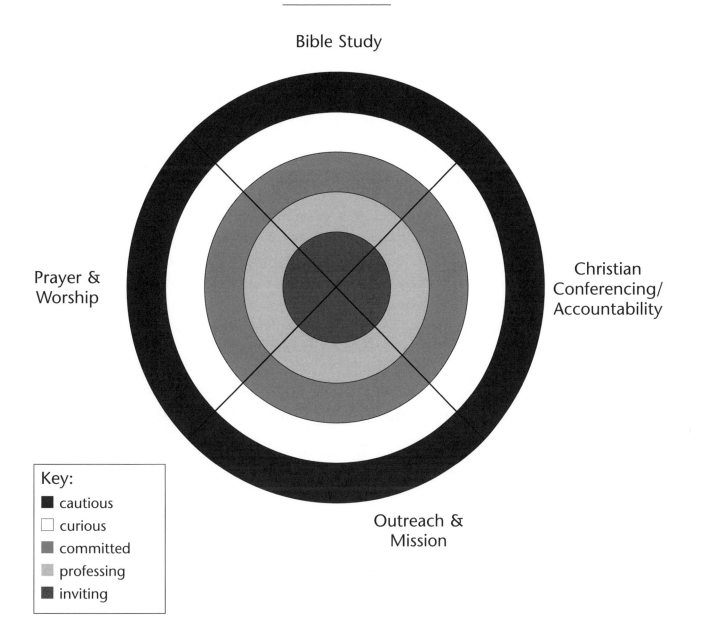

Prayer &
Worship

Christian
Conferencing/
Accountability

Key:
- ■ cautious
- □ curious
- ■ committed
- ■ professing
- ■ inviting

Outreach &
Mission

Whatever tool you develop, it should include the following:

- Ways to include people at any stage of faith development.

- Indications that people move through a process throughout their life. Faith formation is continuous.

- Practices of faithful disciples (including practices of the Wesleyan heritage).

Once you complete your tool framework, you will want to place your church's current ministries for disciple formation within your tool. To place those ministries, match ministries with the practices of faith. You'll also need to identify the stage at which someone might engage in that ministry. Find where those points (practices and stages related to the ministry) converge, and add that ministry's name to your chart, graph, grid, circle, or other tool. For example, your congregation may be using DISCIPLE I as a ministry. Here's how it would fit into the first tool:

|  | Cautious | Curious | Committed | Professing | Inviting |
|---|---|---|---|---|---|
| Inviting |  |  |  |  |  |
| Welcoming |  |  |  |  |  |
| Nurturing |  |  |  | DISCIPLE I |  |
| Sending |  |  |  |  |  |

As you can see, DISCIPLE I aids in the nurturing of Christians, and is a way in which the church currently engages a Professing person (one who knows what it means to serve Christ, uses his/her spiritual gifts for ministry, and who wants to grow in his/her knowledge of the Bible and significant relationships). Continue to place ministries throughout your tool. Note that not every ministry identified throughout the interviewing and listing process will fit into a category.

Once you've completed this task, you will have a good overview of what the church currently does to form disciples. As you complete this process, it is important that you celebrate the ministries you currently have to form disciples. Find a way of marking those ministries – a display, a newsletter article, a time of prayer for them during worship – and showing the congregation and ministry leaders that those ministries have been appreciated.

Now be sure you work back through and in the new dreams to fill the gaps. How will you serve the people you are not yet serving? How will you care for people at various levels of the discipleship process? Plug in the ministries that will fill the gaps.

Don't forget the "Guidelines for a Healthy Disciple-Formation Process" listed at the end of this chapter.

(Handout)

## CHAPTER 6 BIBLE STUDY

# NICODEMUS

Let's trace the faith development of Nicodemus in the gospel of John. John 3:1-21 tells of his first encounter with Jesus. You'll notice that Nicodemus, though he is a Pharisee, holds Jesus in some amount of high regard already, since he refers to him as "Rabbi". Yet Nicodemus doesn't understand who Jesus is and what his kingdom work is about. John 7:45-52 demonstrates some growth in Nicodemus. He asks a tough question of the Pharisees; and in asking that question, he shows that his faith in Jesus is growing. Near the end of the gospel (John 19:38-42), Nicodemus arrives after Jesus' death, bringing items to prepare the body. He and Joseph of Arimathea prepare and wrap the body, and lay it in the tomb. As you reflect on these passages, you might use the following questions to guide discussion and reflection:

1.  In the first passage, Nicodemus has an interest in Jesus and his ministry, but he's unable to give up what he knows (the law). Have you experienced a time in your discipleship journey when you struggled with following Jesus?

2.  In the second passage, Nicodemus has grown stronger in his beliefs about Jesus. He is willing to stand up and defend Jesus. When have you taken a step forward in faith?

3.  In the last passage, Nicodemus has a full understanding of who Jesus is, and how that affects him. He is no longer afraid to demonstrate his faith. As you think back over your faith journey, was there a time when you fully understood who Jesus is? What difference did that make in how you live your life?

4.  Can you see Nicodemus' forward progression throughout the gospel of John? What does that tell you about discipleship?

(Handout)

# GUIDELINES FOR A HEALTHY DISCIPLE-FORMATION PROCESS

- Every disciple-formation process should carry out the church's mission and help to lead your congregation toward attaining God's vision.

- Disciple-formation processes require various entry points into the process, since persons may enter the disciple-formation process at various points on their faith journey.

- Healthy disciple-formation processes focus on the faith journey of individuals and the congregation. They focus on lifelong formation, rather than on programs that provide quick fixes. Periodic Bible studies on Jesus' work with the disciples, his encounter with Nicodemus, or the Ephesians' growth to maturity may aid in helping people understand the need for lifelong formation.

- Because being a disciple is a lifelong journey, a healthy disciple-formation process will include faith-forming ministries for all ages, including children and youth.

- Because human beings develop their faith at different rates, levels or stages are important to a successful disciple-formation process. See Understand Levels and Stages on pages 44-45 to gain more insight and examples of levels and stages.

- Healthy disciple-formation processes will incorporate some aspect of our Wesleyan heritage (kinds of grace, practicing the means of grace, acts of piety/mercy, following the General Rules, etc.)

- Practices will provide guidelines for those engaged in the disciple-formation process. Practices of faith, means of grace, and the church-owned definition of disciple will become the developing guidelines for what it means to grow in faith. Henry Knight's book, *Eight Life-Enriching Practices of United Methodists* (Nashville: Abingdon, 2001) may help you discover practices that are important to your congregation. You may also want to refer to the article "Creating a Discipleship Process for Youth and Young Adults," found in *Making God Real for a New Generation*, by Craig Kennet Miller and MaryJane Pierce Norton (Nashville:

Discipleship Resources, 2003). Pages 131-132 address practices for youth and young adults.

• Every process needs to have identified resources that can help individuals move from stage to stage, increasing the flow of intentional growth.

• Healthy disciple-formation processes include periodic assessments for individuals, the church, and the process itself.

• Disciple-formation processes need an image or metaphor to aid in the process. It may help give voice to stages, practices, visual pictures, and help people grasp the concept of discipleship as a lifelong journey.

• Every disciple-formation process must be relevant to the context in which the congregation engages in ministry.

# WHO'S GOING WITH US?

The desired result for this chapter is to develop the plan to invite persons to own and engage in the congregation's disciple-formation process. It is critical that the various stages of preparing for the disciple-formation process be communicated to the congregation at every phase. Unless the congregation has been involved in the stages up to this point, this step will be difficult, at best, to engage the congregation in the disciple-formation process. However, if the vision has been cast clearly and often, throughout small groups as well as to the congregation as a whole, this next step will seem very natural.

## Centering Prayer

*Ever-faithful God, you have guided us through the development of a disciple-formation process, and we have heard your voice. We have sought to be faithful in visibly laying out your design for disciple formation. As we bring this new disciple-formation process to the congregation and seek to implement it, may you open their hearts and minds to the possibility and challenge of lifelong formation. May the power of your Holy Spirit blow through this team and this congregation, allowing us to hear and heed your call to be faithful disciples. We pray in the name of the one who said "Come, follow me;" Jesus the Christ. Amen.*

## Chapter at a Glance

### GOALS

- Develop the part of the disciple-formation process that invites individuals to engage personally in strengthening their own faith journey

### TIMEFRAME SUGGESTIONS

The timeframe needed here depends on how some other components of the planning process has gone for your team. In order for this part to be implemented effectively and successfully, the other goals must be in place; i.e.,:

- The vision must have been initially and continually cast to the congregation from the beginning, and at this point in time, there should be strong involvement and buy-in from the congregation

- The various levels and stages of disciple formation must have been communicated at each appropriate phase, and individuals should have an understanding of these stages, and should have thoughts about where he/she is in their discipleship journey

- The congregation should be been involved in the developing of the disciple-formation process, as a whole, and in study/dialogue in small groups, and other forms of communication as is relevant in your congregation

- The congregation should be "on board" with the evaluation and discernment of the various activities and ministries in the church, and have an understanding of the importance of the connection between the activity and the mission to make disciples of Jesus Christ

- If some of these components are missing, or you feel they are weak, you will want to pause at this point and do some additional work in those weak areas before your proceed

### POSSIBLE FORMAT

- Read the centering prayer together, or have the facilitator read while the group meditates.

- Review again the mission of your church, in whatever way you think most appropriate.

- Share with the team that we have reached the point in the disciple-formation process when we begin to communicate to the congregation more specific ways in which this applies to each individual; how each person can determine where s/he is on the discipleship journey, and find ministries within your church that will help take him/her to the next stage in their journey. You are now developing strategies to extend that invitation and encouragement to each individual person, so that each one will be involved in deepening his/her faith.

- Some questions for the team:

  - How will we communicate and launch the new disciple-formation process?

  - What has already been communicated to your congregation?

  - How does the individual invitation to grow in discipleship need to be extended, in a way that it is seen as ongoing, not a "one-shot deal"?

  - What is your metaphor for the disciple-formation process, and how will it be used?

  - When and how will the new disciple-formation process begin, or will it be "phased in"? This should be seen by your congregation as a "new day," a "new direction in forming disciples;" that this is the way our congregation will live together from here on, this is not a "start and stop" program that will end in a few months. How do we communicate and integrate that into the life of the congregation?

  - How will you allow for varied entry points so that persons can enter the process at different places and in different ways?

  - How will you share the ways and places people can step into the process?

  - How will you give clear and varied ways people can become involved?

  - How will you include children and youth to be involved in the disciple-formation process in ways that are appropriate for their age level?

  - How will you help the congregation understand the difference between the current reality (individual and communal) and the new future?

- How will you develop ways to invite those from outside the church to be a part of your disciple-formation process?

- Who will be responsible for the various aspects of communication, casting the vision, and launching the new disciple-formation process?

- What loose ends do we have that we need to tie up?

• Close in prayer, in whatever way seems appropriate.

## Individual Preparation

How's your vision statement and disciple-formation process coming along? You prepared it carefully as the result of a lot of hard work on the part of those who have been part of its development. You've evaluated it (and probably modified it) against some insights and standards developed by persons well experienced in this area. And you're feeling pretty good about it. Great! Build on that enthusiasm. Don't let it waver; keep it going! The more each person in your group is excited about your disciple-formation process, the more possibility of that vision statement being reached.

(Here's a subtle way to measure that enthusiasm. Some call it the "parking lot test." What do folks who have been part of your group do when your group meetings have ended? Do they gather up their belongings and race home? Or do they linger, either in the building or in the church parking lot, talking, discussing ideas, sharing insights, building on plans, using their imaginations? The more folks linger to talk together after meetings such as you've been having, the more enthusiasm and excitement about the whole project there will be! One pastor had to start flashing the parking lot lights about an hour after the group meetings ended in order to break up the conversations going on in the parking lot. That's enthusiasm that spills over and builds on itself!)

But (and isn't there always a "but" with these kinds of projects?) the enthusiasm of the folks that have been part of your meetings and conversations is not going to carry the day by itself. One of the next big tasks before you is to get the whole congregation "on board"— to help them discover that the vision your group has developed is not the vision of only a handful of folks in the church (or even worse, the pastor's), but that it is, or can be, the vision of the entire congregation! Let's face it: Unless the whole congregation is behind efforts to fulfill that vision, that mission to make disciples of Jesus Christ, that vision statement is just so many nice words on so many sheets of paper.

Life has to be breathed into the words of the vision statement, and that life comes only when the whole congregation becomes excited about that vision. Remember that great passage from 2 Timothy 3:16? The verse starts out, "All Scripture is inspired by God." But some of the modern translations read, "All Scripture is *breathed upon* by God." What happened when God breathed on a handful of dust, as reported in Genesis 2:7? That dust became alive, became a human being! And what happened when God breathed on the dry bones in Ezekiel 37? The bones began to live!

That's what must happen with your vision statement. It must come alive. It must be breathed upon by God through prayer, and it must come alive through the enthusiasm of the whole congregation. Every member and constituent (a constituent is a person who attends your church on a regular or irregular basis but who is not formally a member) must give life to that vision statement by their enthusiasm, their excitement, and, perhaps most important, their sense of ownership of that vision statement. In other words, each person connected with your congregation must feel that this vision statement is her or his vision statement for the congregation! Nothing can kill a vision more quickly that folks feeling that the vision statement has been laid upon them by someone or something else.

Now if your entire congregation (note that word "entire") has been involved in developing your vision statement, then you can skip this chapter; everybody is already on board! (Everybody? Well, probably not every single person who is connected with your congregation. Every congregation has a few persons who dig in their heels and don't want to move off dead center, who don't want to risk anything new, and who think things are fine just as they are. So "everybody" in this case means the great majority of members of your congregation—such a majority that the naysayers will be swept along in the enthusiasm and excitement of everyone else!)

But if your congregation is like most congregations, you've had only a part of your congregation involved in the development of your disciple-formation process so far. Whatever the case, the next step in implementing this process is *involving the whole congregation* in getting enthusiastic about the vision and plan, and in "tweaking" the plan a bit. "Tweaking?" That simply means modifying, adjusting, perfecting, or editing the vision. And that "tweaking" process is an ongoing process. The vision statement is never absolutely perfect; it is always subject to change and modification. Your congregation's vision statement is not written in concrete or carved on stone; it is written in pencil, and it shows the smudges of many erasures and write-overs. It is a living vision statement!

OK. One of your big tasks now—not *your* as in one individual but *your* as in all of you who have been involved in this visioning process so far – is getting the entire congregation excited about the vision! Some folks have said you have to "sell" the vision, you have to get the rest of the congregation to "buy into" the vision. If terms like that are comfortable for you, fine. But basically what you folks on the team are going to do is generate excitement about that vision.

And you do this through *communication*. A simple word, but sometimes difficult to do, and one that can create problems if you're not careful. A simple word, *communication*, but a key word here.

With whom is communication necessary in this case?

That's easy. Everybody.

On to the next step.

Not so fast! Go back to that word *everybody*! What does that mean? Just what it says. *Everybody* is anyone connected in any way with your congregation. Everybody is the shut-ins and toddlers. Everybody is the youth away at college and that person who never comes to church even though that person's spouse is an active member. Everybody is the teenagers and the "golden agers." Everybody is folks who never miss a Sunday at church and the folks who show up at Easter and around Christmas. Everybody is that family that sort of "dropped out" of the congregation about a year ago but that has not since connected firmly with another congregation. Everybody is children, youth, adults. Everybody includes members who live at far distances but who retain an interest in your congregation.

Now if you are intent on sharing the vision with everybody and collecting everybody's ideas about, reactions to, and tweaking of the vision, then you cannot rely on one or two means or forms of communication. You have to use every means at your disposal!

Stop right now and list all the forms of communication available to your congregation. Here are some ideas to get you started:

- The monthly newsletter
- The Sunday worship bulletins
- The local radio station
- The announcement time that precedes the service of worship.
- That bulletin board that never gets changed or updated in the narthex (that's the

church word for the entry way or vestibule just outside your sanctuary).

- The local newspaper

- The telephone chain or tree (One person calls five designated persons with a message. Each one of those five calls another five designated persons. Each of them calls another five, and so on until everyone has been contacted by telephone. Yes, you can purchase special telephone equipment that will contact every telephone number in your membership and constituent list with a recorded message and even leave that message if no one answers. But most small membership congregations do not have access to such equipment.)

- Your church web site and e-mail lists

- The bulletin board out on the highway that points to your church building

Keep going. Add as many other ways as you can.

Right! We haven't listed sermons! We haven't listed Sunday School teachers and United Methodist Youth Fellowship leaders! We haven't listed special mailings or brochures!

Keep going. Keep going. What other means of communication are available to you and your congregation?

Is one way more important than another way? Is the sermon the best way to get folks excited? Is the newsletter? Is an insert in the worship bulletin?

You know the answer to that by now. It takes all these ways (and more!) to bring the entire congregation on board. It takes all these ways (and more!) to get everybody excited about the vision! It takes all these ways (and more!) to harness the potential, energy, enthusiasm, excitement, and wit in your congregation.

But there is one "most important" way to communicate. Look to the Scriptures for an insight into that special way. Of course we're talking about one-on-one conversation. Nothing is more successful than personal sharing. Nothing is more important that those face-to-face conversations in the church parking lot, over a cup of coffee on Thursday morning, in the check-out line at the grocery store, at the post office, or on the third tee at the golf course, or where ever and whenever persons connected with your congregation come together.

And who are the key persons in those one-on-one conversations? Look back to the group with which you started this disciple-formation process. The folks who worked on definitions, who identified the "things' your congregation does, who formed and shaped the vision statement. But these folks are not promoting their ideas or suggestions; they're not trying to get others to agree with them. If they are communicating effectively, they are excited about the mission of the congregation and the ways your congregation wants to carry out that mission. They are so excited about that mission that they talk of it where ever they are, and soon everyone in the congregation is talking about that mission.

What was that mission of the Church again? Right! To make disciples of Jesus Christ!

One more point about bringing the whole congregation on board: As the television comedians says, "Timing is everything!" And "timing" is important in involving the whole congregation in your planning a vision.

Meaning what?

Meaning simply this: Allow enough time for everybody (there's that *everybody* again!) to have input into the vision statement, but at the same time, do not drag out the communication process. Communicate, tell the story, relate the vision statement, talk about the disciple-formation process, proclaim the excitement about the mission statement, but know when to stop talking and start doing! In other words, focus enough time on this communication phase to be sure the congregation is of one mind, but not so much time in talking that persons get tired of hearing about the vision and begin to think of it as "old hat." You will have a narrow window of time in which to move from talking about the vision to fulfilling the vision. Miss that window by being too early, and you'll not have a unified congregation. Miss that window by being too late, and you'll have a congregation that has become bored with talk and has moved on to other matters.

If only a magic wand existed that could tell us exactly when enough is enough! But since no such thing exists, use the next best thing you have: the other side of communication. The other side? Yes. The other side of communication is *listening*. The entire team that worked on putting together the original vision statement needs to be listening, attuned to what's going on in the congregation. Listening to conversations before and after worship. Listening to conversations in Sunday School classes. Listening to folks chatting in the parking lot. Listening carefully, intently. Is enthusiasm for the mission of the congregation and enthusiasm for your congregation's vision statement growing? Is increased excitement evident? Good! Now is the time to move onto the next phase, to take the next giant step in making disciples of Jesus Christ in and through your congregation!

A caution: If folks are no longer talking much about the mission and vision; if folks have turned to other topics in their informal conversations; if the parking lot and the hallway and the narthex no longer resonate with chatter about the mission and the vision statements, then you might have missed the best moment. Recapture it and move to the next step quickly but carefully!

Remember, remember, remember: This is not *your* vision for *your* mission. This must always be seen by the entire congregation as *our* vision for *our* mission!

## The Role of the Team

At this point, the team has the responsibility for developing the specific plans for all the areas discussed above, and to implement those plans. They are responsible for communicating all this to the entire congregation, as well as inviting and effectively receiving and nurturing individuals as they step into the process. They will need to be active listeners at this point as they detect gaps, confusion, resistance, etc., and work toward positive solutions. One or more persons on the Team needs to be especially attentive to the emotional climate. The team also needs to cover this implementation process with prayer.

## The Role of the Pastor

The pastor needs to continually cast the vision; to the congregation, to small groups, to individuals, in written and spoken format, in as many ways and forms as possible and as often as possible. The pastor also needs to be attentive at this point to listening to the Team as well as the congregation, and readjusting as necessary. With the Team, the pastor needs to continually cover this implementation process with prayer.

## The Role of the Congregation

The congregation needs to be open to what is being shared; obviously, part of the role of the Team is to help prepare a climate for this openness. The congregation should also have opportunity to give feedback at this point, and to participate in the small group sessions, the opportunities for learning about discipleship, and, ultimately, making the decision to enter the discipleship process.

## Check the Emotional Climate

This is where the paradigm shift actually begins to happen. Most likely, the team has spent weeks, perhaps months, reaching this point where the congregation becomes fully involved and engaged, and all the planning and development is now coming to life. The team may be experiencing multiple emotions; excitement, success, momentum, or confusion, disappointment, rejection, or any combination of these and other emotions, depending on how the invitation is going, and how the congregation is responding. There may be parts of the disciple-formation process that the team now sees will not work, and some adjustments may be necessary. This can create tension and frustration. This is a time when some regrouping of the team may be needed; factions can arise, and the Team needs to experience unity. The team will need to be guided to stay focused on the purpose, and not get caught up "majoring in minors."

The team may also grow impatient with the amount of time it will take to move the congregation to align with the vision.

The team needs to make it a priority to allow time for the strengthening of the Team and the refocusing as individuals and for the Team as a whole.

It is also essential that the church, as a whole, understand that disciple formation, for all of us, is a lifelong journey. It is recommended that the congregation become involved in a short-term Bible Study on the journey of one of the well-known disciples of Christ, or Moses, or Abraham, etc., to fully gain understanding of how we grow continually toward the likeness of Christ. We never just "arrive."

## Going Deeper

### Communicating the Vision

This is just one of many places where you've been guided to "communicate the vision." This must be done diligently, often, in many places, and in many ways. Some have said that to communicate effectively, one must share with people seventeen different times and in seventeen different ways before the process has been adequately communicated. This can't be overly emphasized; if the vision is not successfully communicated, the goal will not be reached.

As the vision is being created and recreated at this point, consider using multiple avenues for communication, such as:

- Email

- Visuals

- Bulletin boards

- Flyers

- Newspaper

- Articles in the church newsletter

- Special newsletter on process opportunities

- Bulletin

- Website, or web page on church's website

- Hearing from the leadership

- The pastor – from the pulpit, meetings, writings

- A sermon series

- Telling stories of what is possible

- Giving a united message, if multiple pastors,

- Other church leadership

Also consider the following:

- Help the congregation understand this is an ongoing process; not a one-time plan

- To truly communicate, consider the need to be able to sing, dance, sculpt, speak, and write about the process

- The disciple-formation process needs to become a genetic fabric of the congregation

- Share the "why we're doing this" over and over

- Hear testimonies from people who are growing as disciples (building on the "why we are doing this")

## Implementing the Process

To create momentum, interest, and commitment for the disciple-formation process, there should be a push, a beginning point. This is a point in time where the church recognizes and makes the commitment to, from this time forward, embrace a focus and emphasis on intentional disciple formation. A word of caution as you plan your implementation: this event should be communicated as the beginning point of a new direction, not the beginning of an "event" that will come and go. Make it clear that intentional disciple formation is about to become an integral part of your church from now on, and this marks the beginning point of this new emphasis.

Given the above, a comprehensive implementation plan should be developed, including but certainly not limited to:

- A kickoff event (discipleship fair, dinner, picnic, worship service, etc.)
- Flyers
- Announcements
- Newsletter articles
- Visual aids
- PowerPoint presentation
- Sharing in worship
- Small group activities
- Children's Sunday School and/or groups/activities

Be sure to include people outside the Team itself to participate in the promotion of the disciple-formation plan, so there is not an "inner circle" perspective, but that the congregation feels this is for everyone.

As you implement your process, aso create a way to invite people into the disciple-formation process. This should not be set up so that if an individual missed the implementation, they can't participate. The disciple-formation process should be created so that anyone can enter at any point at any time. The launch just raises awareness of a new beginning.

## The Process of Assessing

In order for people to be able to grow in their discipleship walk, they should understand where they are on that journey. While there are not easily defined "stages" of discipleship, and where we are on our discipleship journey may vary from time to time, a self-awareness is important if people are going to be able to know how to take the next step on the path. This awareness will also help individuals understand the need for continual growth.

It is also important that the opportunity for self-awareness be presented in a non-judgmental way, so individuals don't consider themselves at a "good place" or "bad place" on the journey, just an understanding of where they are.

At this point, you are encouraged to consider creating a format for all small groups in the life of your congregation to be working through at the same time, asking questions such as:

Where am I in my faith development and personal discipleship?
How do I move to the next step?
How is God asking me to help others move?

When helping individuals to assess where they are, guard against the idea that this is a "self-improvement project," but rather a commitment to take a step closer to Christ in the journey of faith.

At this step, and at all steps of inviting individuals to join the disciple-formation process, make participation easy. This is not intended to be a screening device or to test the perseverance of the faithful, but an opportunity for any individual, regardless of where s/he is to take a step deeper as a disciple.

## Additional Resources

Slaughter, Mike. *Real Followers* (Nashville: Abingdon Press, 1999). Rev. Slaughter is the senior pastor Ginghamsburg United Methodist Church in Tipton, Ohio. The story of the growth and transformation of Ginghamsburg is amazing in itself, but the book's underlying theme asks what it means to be a real follower of Jesus, and gives valuable insight to a congregation involved in an intentional disciple-formation process.

## Stages and Assessment

A variety of self-assessment tools are available or you can create your own. A couple suggestions:

www.powerus.org: Christ and Riverside United Methodist Churches, East Moline, Illinois

Spiritual Disciplines Assessment Pack: from *Building Church Leaders,* Leadership Resources, 2003 Christianity Today Int'l

# Before Moving On

- • Determine where you think you have gaps or weak spots in the development, implementation and/or effectiveness of the disciple-formation process. Make plans on how to address these weak spots.

# KEEP IT GOING!

## Centering Prayer

*Merciful God, we pray that we've been faithful to you. As we review our disciple-formation process, the spiritual growth of individuals and the congregation, and ongoing leader formation, keep us mindful of the vision you set before us. May the Church's mission be the measuring stick by which we evaluate the disciple-formation process. We pray that through this process, you have made disciples who continually grow in loving you and their neighbors. If we have made mistakes, please forgive us, and help us find ways that we can continually improve and refine this disciple-formation process to make it what you desire. In the name of Christ we pray, amen.*

## Chapter at a Glance

### GOAL

- To develop an ongoing plan for keeping your new disciple-formation process alive, vital, healthy, and relevant for many years to come

## TIMEFRAME SUGGESTIONS

Be cautious not to skim over this part. This may be multiple sessions; you may hold one session to understand the concepts and intent of the chapter, and then you may want to wait a few weeks to have a few more sessions to determine how to best structure this. If you do not intentionally develop this last piece, you will have a short-lived disciple-formation process, which will be a "program" or "flavor of the month." Your team is tired by now; they may be excited about all that is happening, but without proper attention and future planning, in a few months, much of your hard work will be lost. Take time to really plan for the long-term future of how your congregation makes disciples for Jesus Christ!

## POSSIBLE FORMAT

- Read the centering prayer together, or have the facilitator read while the group meditates.

- Spend some time reviewing where you are at this point (and capture on newsprint):

  - Do you have a comprehensive, intentional, disciple-formation system in place?

  - What is the climate of your congregation around this new direction?

  - What have been some of your pitfalls?

  - How have you overcome those pitfalls?

  - What obstacles are you still trying to overcome?

  - What suggestions do you have for overcoming them?

- Help the team look toward the future:

  - What aspects of the disciple-formation process will need more attention in the near future? How will we provide that?

  - How do we structure our leadership so that every year the disciple-formation process is evaluated, and necessary changes/adjustments are made?

    — Will this disciple-formation process continue to be monitored and improved by a team such as the one that has developed the initial process?

— If so, how do we invite new leadership so the initial team doesn't "burn out" and lose energy through fatigue, while also inviting new ideas and perspectives?

— How often should the team meet to keep the disciple-formation process strong and vital?

— Who should lead the team?

— If we decide not to use a team to monitor this, what process will we use that will be effective?

■ How will we continue to "cast farther out" in terms of our ideal vision? For example, in developing this process, we asked the question, "what would our church be doing five years from now . . . ." As time goes on, how do we continually recast that vision, so we're always looking five more years out (or whatever number of years you decide)?

■ What else needs to be done now to improve the disciple-formation process?

■ Discuss how you will evaluate your disciple-formation process in the future:

— How will you know when you are no longer making disciples?

— How will you know when you are?

— How will you know when you need to suspend a ministry?

— How will we change with our ever-changing congregation?

— How will we recognize and be open to new opportunities that we should pursue?

— How will we continually be searching for God's direction concerning our disciple-formation process?

• Consider ways your team can give thanks to God for allowing them to have a part in the development of this disciple-formation process; allow team members to share ways their own faith has grown through this experience.

• Make **specific** plans for next steps in the ongoing leadership of the disciple-formation process in your congregation. Consider using the handout on p. 117 for further reflection and development of your ongoing plan for evaluation.

• Close in prayer, in whatever way seems appropriate.

# Individual Preparation

So you've had a success. Great! Celebrate it! Build on it! Don't stop now; you're on a roll!

You've learned that the mission of the Church is to make disciples of Jesus Christ.

You've defined just what a disciple is, and you've evaluated your present ministries in terms of their disciple-making potentials.

You've looked into the future and decided what you as a congregation want to be doing about making disciples in the future. And you've successfully involved the whole congregation in the enthusiasm of disciple-making ministries.

You have commenced some new disciple-making ministries, and perhaps let go of some things, all to the end of making and forming disciples of Jesus Christ. And the whole congregation is excited about the future. You and your congregation are going to be involved in the task of making disciples! Several thinkers have reminded us that the church is one of the few organizations that focuses more on those who are not members of the organization than on the members of the organization. That's because our task, our mission, is to make disciples. We'll keep checking to see if we're faithful to that task.

A note of reality and humility here: We do not "make" disciples. No congregation "makes" disciples. The Lord God makes disciples when persons hear God's call and claim on their lives and when these persons respond in faith and trust to that call and that claim. Therefore, no congregation can ever "chalk one up" and say, "There. We've made a disciple." We will continually evaluate if we are doing our part in disciple making. What congregations do is to provide the settings, the situations, the environments, and the opportunities in and through which persons can hear, experience, and respond to God's call and claim with a commitment to become part of the covenant community.

Why emphasize this? Because the glory is not ours; it is God's. The achievement is not ours; it is God's. The success is not ours; it is God's. But because you and your congregation have decided in new and definite ways to provide those occasions in and through which persons can respond to God's claim on their lives, you are making disciples by being disciples. Beware the church members who proudly boast, "We are making disciples because we are doing this or that." Instead, proclaim in all humility that "God may be using us and the ministries we have put in place so that others may come to know God through Christ. To God be the glory!"

That being said, let's summarize this disciple-formation process with a couple of points for possible discussion.

You've had some successes. You started that new young adult Sunday School class. You involved the children from the public housing project in your Vacation Bible School. You set up that 24/7/365 prayer line staffed by older persons in their homes through the telephone company's ability to transfer calls. You are truly becoming an outward looking congregation rather than a congregation that focuses only on "maintenance;" that is, paying the bills and keeping the doors open for the members.

So how do you keep this enthusiasm going?

A couple of ways.

Never be afraid to try a new ministry of disciple making, no matter how extreme it might seem to some at the beginning. The gospel of Jesus Christ is extreme! It's radical! Yes, offering the use of your church building on Sunday afternoons to the struggling congregation that speaks a different language might result in fingerprints on the walls and occasional strange smells in the kitchen. But so what? You're providing a place and setting where disciple making can take place. "But those folks will never join our church." You're probably right. But your mission is not to build up your own local church with more and more people; your mission is to make disciples!

Disciples of First United Methodist Church? No.

Disciples of the United Methodist denomination? No.

Disciples of Jesus Christ? Yes! A resounding yes!

And the flip side of that caveat is equally important.

*Never be afraid to suspend a ministry that is simply not working.* Never be afraid to decide that the expenditure of persons, resources, and energy on a particular ministry is not paying off. One of the biggest problems we have in many congregations is not starting new ministries, but not knowing how to stop them when they prove unfruitful. So what do we do instead? We try to repair a ministry that is not working by pumping more energy and resources into it as if that would help. Or, even worse, we try to make folks feel guilty for not supporting that ministry. And we all know what effect inducing guilt on others, and on ourselves, has.

So let some ministries die. Give them a decent funeral. Rejoice at what you learned from failed efforts. And forge ahead in a new direction!

How do you know when a ministry is on its last legs? When only a few in the congregation cling to it; when enthusiasm for it wanes, when you have to beg folks to take part rather than trying to find places of service within it for all who are anxious to volunteer for it.

And, most important, when it is no longer making disciples.

How do you know when it is not making disciples? When it is no longer reaching out to the community and when it is no longer strengthening the faith and the discipleship of those already within the congregation. When it is appealing only to members of the congregation, and when only the same handful of members of the congregation continue to take part.

You may be getting the idea here that evaluating disciple-making ministries in your congregation is difficult. Yes, it is. But this is an area where each of us needs to get our own opinions and ideas out of the way and focus on the mission of the Church. Yes, a particular idea may be our pet project. We may be excited about it. We may have invested a lot of energy into getting it up and running. But at the same time we need to remember that when we share an idea with a group, that idea is no longer ours; it is the group's. And it is the group, not we as individuals, who have the responsibility of determining when a ministry is making disciples and when it is not.

Another way of saying this is that making disciples is more important than any one of us or our individual ideas. Making disciples is what we as the body of Christ, the church, do. And we can do infinitely more together than we can do individually. So forget whose idea a new ministry is; get behind it and support it. If it succeeds in making disciples, rejoice! If it does not, change it or leave it and move on to another ministry that promises greater success.

Keep that enthusiasm, not for a particular ministry but for the mission of the congregation, going and growing by realizing that the congregation is a living organism.

Wow! What's that mean?

Simply this: Although we trust the stability of God's presence with us and around us, we know that a congregation is an ever-changing, every-becoming reality. The congregation of which we are a part today is not the same congregation of which we were a part last year or last month or last week, and is not the same congregation of which we will be a part next year or next month or next week. Just like many other organisms, congregations start to die when they stand still. Congregations begin to wither when they cease to change and grow, not just numerically, but also spiritually and in terms of discipleship. Congregations start a downward spiral when they refuse to recognize that change is inevitable.

One way to maintain enthusiasm for disciple-making ministries is to recognize that your congregation is an ever-changing, ever-becoming reality. It will never again be as it was at some time in the past; trying to return to what it was back there and then is a sure way to begin that downward spiral.

Disciple-making congregations embrace change—new opportunities, new potentials, new possibilities, new ideas, new ministries!

Disciple-making congregations maintain enthusiasm for making disciples because folks can't wait to discover what new disciple-making ministries are in the works!

Disciple-making congregations discover new ideas for disciple-making ministries all throughout the congregation. Ideas are not the providence of the designated leaders or the official bodies of the church. Ideas are generated throughout the congregation, and every idea is treated with enthusiasm and respect.

Disciple-making congregations are restless congregations, in the very best sense of the word. They are restless in that they do not rest on past achievements. Restless in that they are eager to try something new and different to make disciples. Restless in that each member of the congregation is growing in faith and discipleship, and because each member is growing in faith and discipleship, the whole congregation is always standing on tiptoe to see new ways to make disciples.

And finally, disciple-making congregations are congregations that live in the here and now and know full well that all that they need for the future is already within the congregation today. Disciple-making congregations are congregations who no longer make excuses. They no longer said, "If only . . ." or "We can't because . . ." Disciple-making congregations plumb the depths of the talents and skills already resident in the congregation. Disciple-making congregations expect every member and constituent to offer her or his best to the task of making disciples.

In a recent book titled *God's Politics*, Jim Wallis, the author, titled his Epilogue, "We Are the

Ones We've Been Waiting For." That holds especially true for congregations that seriously seek to become disciple-making congregations. Those congregations long ago quit saying, "If only we could get some new folks," or "We need to get more active members in our church." Disciple-making congregations are those congregations who know how to utilize every member and constituent of the congregation for the purpose of making disciples of Jesus Christ. Disciple-making congregations know that making disciples is their task, not someone else's. Disciple-making congregations focus all their energy and resources, past, present, and future, to the task of making disciples.

For that, and that alone, is the reason congregations exist.

Jesus said it: "'Go therefore and make disciples of all nations." (Matthew 28:19)

We sing it: "Go, Make of All Disciples." (#571 in *The United Methodist Hymnal*)

Now let us do it. Our mission is to make disciples of Jesus Christ. Thanks be to God!

And now may the grace of our Lord Jesus Christ be with you all as you seriously embark upon fulfulling the call of the Great Commission.

# Additional Resources

Hudson, Jill. *When Better Isn't Enough* (The Alban Institute, 2004). This book has much information about the evaluation process, from several perspectives, i.e., the pastor, the review committee, the associate pastor, volunteers, etc. She also included the "12 characteristics for effective 21st century ministry."

Hook, M. Anne Burnette and Shirley F. Clement. *Staying Focused: Building Ministry Teams for Christian Formation* (Nashville: Discipleship Resources, 2002). Chapter 4 specifically discusses ways to nurture ministry areas in discipleship formation. Written assessments (individual and congregation) Self assessments (guidelines, examinations, reflection questions)

(Handout)

# ONGOING PLAN FOR EVALUATION

We've prayed, planned implemented, laughed, worked, and watched. Are we making disciples? Are we transforming our community, and the world? Now it's time to take stock, and look at how things are going, and make necessary changes. Our mission won't change. Our vision will continue to evolve as we move forward in fulfilling God's mission for the Church. Despite this, the measure of a healthy disciple-formation process is always "Are we making and forming disciples?"

We build in this evaluation component early so that we can remember what we're evaluating later. In this section we hope to provide tools for you to devise your own evaluation tool.

As you begin to reflect on the process to date, ask the questions:

Are we making disciples?

How do we know?

What have we learned thus far?

How can we evaluate this effectively?

Is subjective evaluation enough?

Are we paying attention to the emotional impact that data can have (differences of opinion, "sacred cows," etc.)

As you process the information from your evaluation efforts, consider where gaps might exist at this point in time. It will be necessary for the team and/or congregation to participate periodically in one or more of the exercises from chapter 4 again to determine the congregation's current reality. Ask together:

What is the difference between our current reality and God's preferred future for our church?

Does our disciple formation process include all the components of a core process (inviting, welcoming, nurturing, sending)?

What is our timeline for gathering data and evaluating on an ongoing basis?

What metrics have we developed/should we develop for evaluating effectively?

When planning for the evaluation piece, consider the main components that have been involved: individuals, the Team, the congregation, and the community.

Questions to consider:

If we've used written individual and/or congregational assessments, what is this information telling us?

What are we hearing when we engage in personal testimonies shared in small groups, during worship time, and during other gatherings?

What sermon series have been used, and what kind of feedback have we received?

Are we inviting people who have yet to make a faith commitment?

Are we celebrating our spiritual growth?

Is the disciple formation process tied to the church-owned definition of disciple?

Is the Team recognizing the affirmations as well as the "uh-ohs"?

Do the people in the community see the church making a difference in the community?

As the team looks back to the brainstorming that was done in chapter 5 about what the church would "look like" if every individual was living as a disciple, reflect on whether the congregation has taken a step closer toward that vision.

Let the team dialogue about how to "measure" discipleship. Be sure there is ongoing communication at every level on what a disciple looks like, how a disciple grows, what the growth expectations are. Develop a metric or tool for the congregation to use to assess communal growth. What intangibles are present that indicate growth?

Be careful that 'fruits' aren't defined by inward or by institutional measures. Ask individuals in small groups to talk about how they see fruits in each other's lives. Build in an ongoing assessment of fruits. Every year, individuals should conduct a self-assessment to see how/where they've grown.

Fresh leadership can be continually transitioned in, roles and responsibilities for leadership should be clear, and evaluations should be ongoing and tied back to the disciple-formation process so that needed adjustments are made as the evaluations indicate. Someone, or perhaps more than one person, needs to have the specific responsibility for monitoring the ongoing progress. In focusing on keeping the momentum strong, consider both quantitative and qualitative data in the evaluation. The grid you have already developed will help at this point. Identify the gaps in the grid, and evaluate how people move from one step to the next in the discipleship journey. But be sure to explore the question "Does every gap have to be filled?" Especially in smaller churches, decide whether one "block on the grid" serves to fill blocks in other areas. Perhaps gaps are filled on rotating basis.

# APPENDIX: COMPREHENSIVE BOOK LIST

*Accountable Discipleship*. Steven W. Manskar (Nashville: Discipleship Resources, 2000).

*A Faithful Future, vol. 2*. Various authors. (Nashville: Discipleship Resources, 2003).

*As if the Heart Mattered*. Gregory S. Clapper (Nashville: Upper Room Books, 1997).

*Devotional Life in the Wesleyan Tradition*. Steve Harper (Nashville: Upper Room Books, 1995).

*Discerning God's Will Together*. Danny E. Morris and Charles M. Olsen (Nashville: Upper Room Books, 1997).

*Growing True Disciples: New Strategies for Producing Genuine Followers of Christ*. George Barna (Colorado Springs: Waterbrook Press, 2001).

*Leading Change*. John Kotter (Boston: Harvard Business School Press, 1996).

*Listening to God*. John Ackerman (Herndon, VA: The Alban Institute, 2001).

*Making God Real for a New Generation*. Craig Kennet Miller and MaryJane Pierce Norton (Nashville: Discipleship Resources, 2003).

*Memories, Hopes, and Conversations*. Mark Lau Branson (Herndon, VA: The Alban Institute, 2004).

*More Ready Than You Realize*. Brian McLaren (Grand Rapids: Zondervan, 2002).

*Practicing Our Faith*. Dorothy C. Bass, ed. (San Francisco: Jossey-Bass, 1997).

*Real Followers*. Mike Slaughter (Nashville: Abingdon Press, 1999).

*Staying Focused: Building Ministry Teams for Christian Formation*. M. Anne Burnette Hook and Shirley F. Clement (Nashville: Discipleship Resources, 2002).

*This Day: A Wesleyan Way of Prayer*. Laurence Hull Stookey (Nashville: Abingdon Press, 2004).

*Transforming Church Boards*. Charles M. Olsen (Herndon, VA: The Alban Institute, 1995).

*Traveling Together: A Guide for Disciple-forming Congregations*. Jeffrey D. Jones (Herndon, VA: The Alban Institute, 2006).

*Way to Live*. Dorothy C. Bass & Don C. Richter, eds. (Nashville: Upper Room Books, 2002).

*When Better Isn't Enough*. Hudson, Jill. Alban Institute (2004)